Resources for
Every Day in Every Way:
A Teacher's Handbook of Preschool Activities

Cynthia Holley and Faraday Burditt

Fearon Teacher Aids
Parsippany, NJ

Simon & Schuster Supplementary Education Group

Illustrator: Duane Bibby
Designer: Bonnie Grover

In memory of my father,
who read me stories,
sang me songs,
and taught me to play
Cindy Holley

To every member of my family,
both young and old,
for their support,
encouragement,
and understanding
Faraday Burditt De la Camara

Contents

Acknowledgments   7

Introduction   9

The Preschool Child   11

What Do We Know about the Preschool Child?   13

What Is the Preschool Child Ready to Learn?   16

How Should the Preschooler Be Taught?   21

The Preschool Program   23

Checklist of General Goals for Early Childhood Programs   25

Checklist for Developing a Preschool Program   26

Classroom Learning Centers   28

Diagnostic Instruments for Young Children   34

Early Warning Signs of Special Needs   39

Background Information Form for Preschool Children   41

Progress Reports for Preschool and Kindergarten   45

Songs, Rhymes, and Fingerplays   57

Recipes for Crafts and Creations   103

Recipes for Snacks and Meals   107

Reproducible Resources   119

Index   220

Acknowledgments

The ideas and activities in *Every Day in Every Way* come from more than 100 sources and over 25 combined years of teaching young children. We wish to give special thanks to the following individuals for their encouragement and suggestions:

Dr. Constance Champlin, Director of Library and Media Services, Indianapolis, Indiana

Dr. John Champlin, Special Education Consultant, Council Bluffs, Iowa

Paloma Garrido, Bilingual Preschool Teacher Assistant, Madrid, Spain

Dorritt Hansen, Preschool Teacher, Copenhagen, Denmark

Constance Johnston, Speech and Language Clinician, Wilmington, Illinois

Sibley Labendiera, Kindergarten Teacher, Madrid, Spain

Diantha McBride, Librarian and Curriculum Coordinator, Madrid, Spain

Trudy Rutherford, Early Childhood Physical Education Specialist, Madrid, Spain

Donna Schreck, School Psychologist, Omaha, Nebraska

Rachel Siebert, Harvard University Doctoral Candidate, Boston, Massachusetts

Karen Walsh, Nutrition Consultant, Virginia Beach, Virginia

We are grateful for permission to include the following selections in this book:

"Bat" (pattern), reprinted from *Holiday Art Projects*, written and illustrated by Jerome C. Brown, Copyright 1984 by David S. Lake Publishers. "My Dreydl," music by S. E. Goldfarb; arranged by Harry Coopersmith; words by S. S. Grossman. Reprinted from *The Songs We Sing*, selected and edited by Harry Coopersmith, Copyright 1950 by The United Synagogue of America, with permission by The United Synagogue of America Commission on Jewish Education. "Progress Report for Preschool" and "Progress Report for Kindergarten," reprinted by permission of The American School of Madrid. "Does Your Child Have Special Needs? Watch for Early Warning Signs," reprinted by permission of Loess Hills Area Education Agency 13, Council Bluffs, Iowa. "Unfortunately," by Bobbi Katz, Copyright 1976, reprinted with permission of the author.

Introduction

Every day more children are attending preschool programs because more mothers are working and because more parents see preschool as an enriching experience that they want to offer their children. With this greater awareness of the benefits of early childhood education, preschool programs have gained a more important place in "academia."

Psychologists, researchers, and child development specialists continue to provide evidence of the influence of environmental factors on the development of young children. It has been reported that as much as half of an individual's intelligence is developed by the age of 4 and that the first 4 or 5 years are the most susceptible to environmental influences. Many leaders in early childhood education see the educational developments in the earliest years of life as the most important and the most in need of attention.

School administrators and early childhood educators have a greater responsibility than ever to reassess the role of early childhood education in the life of young children and the role of the preschool as the first link in a long chain of instruction. Success in a child's progress through school depends largely on the foundation laid in the early years.

This book and its companion volume, *Every Day in Every Way: A Year-Round Calendar of Preschool Learning Challenges,* are designed to help early childhood educators stimulate students of varying backgrounds, ages, and levels of achievement. In this teacher's handbook, you will find a concise but comprehensive description of the developmental skills of preschoolers; use it to gauge the appropriateness of classroom activities. You'll also find helpful checklists of general goals and practical considerations for preschool programs as well as descriptions of a well-rounded variety of learning centers. There is a review of recommended diagnostic instruments for young children (to be used with discretion and with training) and a form to share with parents about early warning signs of special needs. To facilitate recordkeeping, there are reproducible forms for background student information, preschool and kindergarten progress reports, and parent-teacher conferences.

The last half of this teacher's handbook is a comprehensive collection of activities for the preschool classroom: songs, rhymes, fingerplays, recipes (both for crafts and for snacks), and worksheets and patterns. Although all these activities are components of the weekly units in *Every Day in Every*

Way: A Year-Round Calendar of Preschool Learning Challenges, they can also enhance a curriculum of your own design.

All the material in both volumes of *Every Day in Every Way* is the result of the authors' experience at The American School of Madrid, Spain, with children of diverse backgrounds, nationalities, and abilities. Although the topics and materials are most relevant for children in standard preschool, day care, and kindergarten classrooms in the United States, they are also appropriate for bilingual classrooms and for those with children from other cultures. With adjustments for developmental ages, many of the activities can also be used in preschool handicapped and primary special education classrooms. We hope that the ideas and materials presented here will be enjoyable as well as meaningful for your students, and that they will be practical as well as informational for you.

The Preschool Child

A valid preschool program should contribute to all aspects of a child's development: physical, cognitive, language, social, and emotional. No one aspect can be ignored. All the young child's developing potentials should be challenged, exercised, and supported.

Recent studies of child development and the brain have shown that certain skills are learned best at certain stages of development and that the effectiveness of various methods of instruction depends on their appropriateness for each stage. Therefore, a sound preschool curriculum must address the following questions:

1. What do we know about the preschool child?
2. What is the preschool child ready to learn?
3. How should the preschool child be taught?

What Do We Know about the Preschool Child?

According to the renowned child psychologist Jean Piaget, preschoolers are at the preoperational stage of development. They are active learners who gain knowledge by acting directly on and with concrete objects. Through these actions they generate hypotheses, predict outcomes, and draw conclusions about the world.

Young children learn best through playful interaction with their environment. Through repeated activity with concrete objects, 3- to 5-year-olds assimilate new elements into their already formed ideas about reality and accommodate or change these ideas when newly assimilated knowledge causes them to do so. They eagerly engage in symbolic thought by representing ideas and events with words, drawings, and dramatic play. They are egocentric beings and have difficulty seeing the world from any viewpoint but their own.

Preschoolers are constantly in motion and are rapidly gaining control of their bodies. Until now, they have spent most of their time at home and their experience as social beings has been somewhat limited. In preschool most children begin to interact with people outside the family and to learn how to relate and socialize within a group.

It would be difficult to find more avid learners than preschoolers. They are tireless experimenters and investigators. Already problem solvers, they benefit from practice in this skill so that they can acquire the ability to think logically.

During the first years of formal education, a child's thinking is stimulated at all levels, and even preschoolers can be encouraged to think creatively and evaluatively. Preschoolers' language is developing rapidly and can benefit from continued encouragement and guidance. In these early years, educators not only help young children form basic concepts but also nurture creativity. To the preschool child, learning is an exciting endeavor.

The Preschool Child

Cognitively

- likes to be read to
- learns by doing
- needs encouragement to talk and communicate
- is learning how to listen
- enjoys participating in stories and drama
- models language and actions of others
- is curious and creative
- benefits from concrete sensory experiences
- likes to change tasks frequently
- wants to explore and learn

Physically

- has a great need for activity
- needs a balance of rest and activity
- must develop large and small muscles
- is improving eye-hand coordination
- enjoys music and rhythms
- is beginning to use simple tools
- can remain with one task for only a limited time
- should be given time for free play

Emotionally

- needs to know limits and expectations
- should know when a job is well done
- has a great need for security
- needs structure with time for individual needs
- is sensitive to the feelings of others
- thrives in a warm and nurturing environment
- appreciates warmth and encouragement
- needs much success

Socially

- likes to work and play with others
- is learning to care for personal possessions
- is beginning group interactions
- needs to be encouraged to share
- likes to receive praise
- may wish to be alone at times
- enjoys pretending and humor
- may attempt to settle squabbles physically rather than with words
- is beginning to share
- likes to be a part of a group

What Is the Preschool Child Ready to Learn?

Preschool children are ready to acquire many skills. The curriculum must be relevant to their needs and prepare them for future school years. The experience offered to young children should help them increase the skills of problem solving, thinking, reasoning, and creating—not just the skill of memorizing. Preschool children need opportunities for growth and stimulation in all areas of development: physical, language, social, emotional, and mental.

Preschool children must continue to develop control of their bodies and therefore must be encouraged to participate in numerous activities that promote gross and fine motor coordination. Their auditory and visual perception skills also need honing. Ready for increased socialization, preschoolers need to obtain greater awareness of themselves as individuals and as members of society.

Young children are naturally inquisitive and eager to explore, create, and learn. They should be offered abundant opportunities to interact naturally with their environment. Though preschool children can be taught to memorize information such as alphabet letters and sight words, this information will not be meaningful if simply learned through rote drill. Reciting rote responses does not reflect real understanding of the information. For a child to fully comprehend a concept, the information must be meaningful in the context of the child's experience and development. When learning is relevant to the young child, not only is comprehension improved, but motivation to learn more is noted.

An effective preschool curriculum matches the children's level of development. The chart "Developmental Milestones in Early Childhood" indicates the normal sequence of the development of skills. Familiarity with this sequence helps early childhood educators to better understand and have more realistic expectations of the children with whom they work. Use this chart only as a general guideline, however. Each child has unique needs and abilities because each child's experiences and background are unique. No two children will demonstrate the behaviors described in this chart in exactly the same way at exactly the same time.

Developmental Milestones in Early Childhood

The Two-Year-Old

Motor Skills

Runs forward well
Jumps in place, two feet together
Stands on one foot, with aid
Walks on tiptoe
Kicks ball forward
Throws large ball
Stands on one foot momentarily
Balances on balance board momentarily, with both feet
Strings four large beads
Turns pages singly
Snips with scissors
Holds crayon with thumb and fingers, not fist
Uses one hand consistently
Folds paper in half with demonstration
Imitates circular, vertical, horizontal strokes
Paints with some wrist action, makes dots, lines, circular strokes
Rolls, pounds, squeezes, and pulls clay
Constructs with Legos, Tinkertoys, etc.
Turns handle on jack-in-the-box
Clips clothespins on a can

Communication Skills

Points to pictures of common objects
Can identify objects when told their use
Understands negatives such as "no," "can't," "don't"
Enjoys listening to simple storybooks and requests them to be repeated
Repeats two digits in order
Labels common objects and pictures
Joins vocabulary words together in 2- to 3-word phrases
Gives first and last names
Asks "what" and "where" questions
Makes negative statements, such as "Can't open it"
Shows frustration at not being understood
300–400 words in vocabulary

Cognitive Skills

Responds to simple directions, such as "Give me the ball"
Selects and looks at picture books
Names pictured objects
Knows concepts of *one, many*, and *more*
Understands prepositions *to* and *with*
Completes 3-shape formboard
Can nestle cups sequentially
Points to 6 body parts on doll
Groups associated objects, such as cup and saucer
Stacks rings on peg in size order
Recognizes self in mirror
Can talk briefly about what he or she is doing
Imitates adult actions, such as sweeping, ironing
Has limited attention span
Learning is through exploration and adult direction
Is beginning to understand functional concepts of objects, such as "Spoon is for eating"
Is beginning to understand whole-part concepts

Personal-Social Skills

Uses spoon, spilling little
Gets drink from fountain or faucet independently
Opens door by turning handle
Takes off coat
Puts on coat with assistance
Washes and dries hands with assistance
Plays near other children
Watches other children and sometimes joins in their play
Defends own possessions
Begins to play house
Uses objects symbolically
Participates in simple group activities, games, songs
Knows gender
Increasing sense of independence
Generally does as told, or minds
May be afraid of thunder, sirens, loud noises
May enjoy performing for others

SOURCES: Tina E. Banks, *Language and Learning Disorders of the Preacademic Child with Curriculum Guide*, 2d ed. (Prentice-Hall, 1982); Joanne Hendrick, *Total Learning for the Whole Child* (C. V. Mosby, 1975); Beth Langley, *Guidelines for Teachers and Evaluators* (George Peabody College for Teachers, 1976); *Project Memphis: Lesson Plans for Enhancing Preschool Developmental Progress* (Memphis State University, 1976); Anne Sanford, *The Learning Accomplishment Profile* (Chapel Hill, NC, 1974).

The Three-Year-Old

Motor Skills

Walks stairs, holding rail, alternating feet
Runs around obstacles
Balances on one foot for several seconds
Hops on one foot
Pushes, pulls, steers wheeled toys
Rides a tricycle
Uses slide without assistance
Jumps over 6-inch-high object, landing feet together
Throws ball overhead
Catches bounced ball
Fastens snaps
Builds 9- to 12-block tower
Drives nails and pegs
Copies circle
Imitates cross
Rolls and shapes clay forms
Strings 1/2-inch beads
Cuts across a strip of paper
Completes 10-piece formboard

Cognitive Skills

Recognizes and matches 6 colors
Works 3- to 5-piece puzzle
Intentionally stacks blocks or rings by size order
Builds 3-block bridge
Draws a somewhat recognizable picture
Names and briefly explains pictures
Counts 3 objects
Knows gender and age
Knows first and last names
Has short attention span, is easily distracted
Learns through observing and imitating
  adult actions
Has increased understanding of function and
  groupings of objects
Puts two halves together to form a simple picture
Comprehends concept of same-different
Matches geometrical forms
Begins to be aware of the concept of past
  and present

Communication Skills

Begins to understand time concepts, such as
  "Tomorrow we will go to Grandma's house"
Understands "big" and "bigger," "long"
  and "short"
Understands relationships expressed by "if . . . ,"
  "then . . . ," and "because . . . ,"
Carries out a series of 2 to 4 related directions
Understands when told "let's pretend"
Vocabulary of more than 1,000 words
Understands some abstract words
Answers questions
Tells about past experiences
Uses plurals
Uses -ed on verbs to indicate past tense
Uses pronouns I and me to refer to self
Repeats a nursery rhyme; sings a song
Repeats 3 digits in sequence
Speech is understandable to strangers, but
  continues to contain some errors
Sentence length is generally 4 to 5 words
Uses prepositions in, under, and on in syntactical
  structures

Personal-Social Skills

Eats independently with minimal assistance
Brushes hair independently
Pours from pitcher into cup
Spreads butter with knife
Buttons and unbuttons large buttons
Washes hands independently
Uses facial tissue, with reminder
Uses toilet independently (may need assistance
  to clean and dress self)
Puts on shoes and socks (without tying)
Brushes teeth adequately
Joins in play of other children, interacts
Takes turns and shares, with encouragement
Tries to help with chores, such as sweeping
Begins dramatic play, acting out scenes, such
  as babysitting

The Four-Year-Old

Motor Skills

Walks backward, toe-to-heel
Jumps forward 10 times without falling
Walks up and down stairs with alternating feet
Turns somersaults
Gallops
Walks full length of balance beam or walking board
Catches a rolled ball
Cuts continuously on line
Copies cross and square
Prints *V* and *H*
Imitates a 6-cube pyramid
Matches simple parquetry patterns

Communication Skills

Follows 3 unrelated commands in sequence
Understands comparatives like *pretty, prettier, prettiest*
Listens to long stories, but may misinterpret the facts
Incorporates verbal directions into play activities
Understands more abstract words
Understands sequencing of events when told "First we will go to the store, then you can go to play at Billy's house"
Asks "when," "how," and "why" questions
Uses models like *can* and *might*
Joins sentences together
Uses *because* and *so* to indicate causality
Tells content of story, but may confuse facts
Comprehends questions like "What do we do when we're tired?"
Repeats 5-word sentences
Identifies common opposites, such as hot and cold
Comprehends prepositions *at the side of, in front of, between*
Retells a fairy tale in logical sequence

Cognitive Skills

Works puzzles of several pieces (10–14)
Counts 3 items meaningfully
Plays with words: repetitions, rhyming, nonsense words
Points to and names 4 to 6 colors
Matches pictures of familiar objects, such as shoe, foot, and sock
Draws a person with up to 6 recognizable parts
Can name many body parts in picture or on self
Draws, names, and describes a recognizable picture
Counts by rote to 5, and perhaps to 10
Knows own street and town, and perhaps phone number
Understands concept of day and night
Answers questions like "What are your eyes for?"
Has longer attention span
Learns through observing and listening to adults, as well as through exploration
Continues to be easily distracted
Has increased understanding of concepts of function, time, and whole-part relationships
May state function or use of objects in addition to their names
Understands more time concepts, including yesterday, last week, a long time ago
Matches dominoes and lotto cards
Comprehends 1-to-1 correspondence
Identifies number concepts 2 and 3
Matches letter, shape, and number cards

Personal-Social Skills

Cuts easy foods with knife
Laces shoes
Buttons medium to small buttons
Toilets self, including cleaning and dressing
Distinguishes front and back of clothing
Washes face well
Hangs up coat
Engages zipper
Puts toys away, cleans up
Plays and interacts with other children with minimal friction
Dramatic play is closer to reality, with attention to detail, time, and space
Enjoys playing dress-up
Shows interest in exploring gender differences
Separates readily from mother
Uses play materials correctly
Attends well for stories
Enjoys being part of a group
Accepts responsibilities

The Five-Year-Old

Motor Skills

Runs lightly on toes
Walks forward, sideways on balance beam
Can hop for 6 feet, 6 inches
Skips, alternating feet
Jumps rope
Skates
Cuts out simple shapes
Copies triangles
Traces diamond
Copies or writes first name
Prints numerals 1 to 5, and perhaps to 10
Colors within lines
Holds pencil properly
Hand dominance usually established
Pastes and glues appropriately
Copies model of square made with pegs
Awareness of own right and left sides emerging

Communication Skills

Comprehends quantitative adjectives, such as *pair, few, many*
Comprehends verb agreement: *is* and *are*
Occasional grammar errors still noted
Still learning subject-verb agreement and irregular past tense verbs
Language is essentially complete in structure and form, with correct usage of all parts of speech
Can take appropriate turns in a conversation
Communicates well with family, friends, or strangers
Reads by way of pictures
Answers questions directly
Relates fanciful tales in own words

Cognitive Skills

Retells story from picture book with reasonable accuracy
May name some letters and numerals
Counts 10 objects
Sorts objects by size, color, shape
Uses classroom equipment, such as scissors, meaningfully and purposefully
Uses time concepts of *yesterday, today,* and *tomorrow* accurately
Begins to relate clock time to daily schedule
Attention span increases noticeably; is less distractable
Learns through adult instruction as well as through exploration
Concepts of function improve, as well as under standing of why things happen
Completes a puzzle of a person divided into 6 parts
Imitates 2-step triangle fold
Completes sequential block patterns, alternating two blocks of one color with one block of another color
Matches and sorts with paper and pencil, marking the one that does not belong

Personal-Social Skills

Dresses self completely, ties bow
Crosses street safely
Makes simple sandwiches
Can prepare bowl of cereal
Brushes teeth independently, can apply paste
Waters plants
Can make simple purchases
Can assist in making bed, setting table, sweeping
Chooses own friends, may show preference for playmates of the same gender and age
Plays simple table games
Plays competitive games and enjoys sports that require group participation
May be afraid of dogs, of the dark, that mother will not return
Self-centered, with own interests and actions taking precedence
Enjoys make-believe play

How Should the Preschooler Be Taught?

The young child learns through actions on objects and through exploration in the environment. Preschoolers learn best in natural settings that allow them to be active participants. Sound early childhood programs should encourage young children to be

- explorers
- creators
- communicators
- interactors
- questioners
- problem solvers
- thinkers
- reasoners
- socializers.

Preschoolers cannot be "taught" in the traditional sense of the word. They can be stimulated, guided, and encouraged in carefully planned activities that allow them to develop at their own optimum rate. An early childhood educator can provide and arrange for these experiences but must not thrust solutions to problems on the children. They must be allowed to discover the answers themselves through experimentation and investigation.

Information must be learned in a meaningful context to enable full understanding by the young child. The teacher provides the props, experiences, and interactions. The children use all five senses to interact with the objects, people, and events that are presented.

Children learn best when there is a planned curriculum of activities focused on a particular theme or concept. Through the thematic approach, children's experiential base is broadened and their mental schemata is increased. This schemata is one of the keys to learning how to read.

Every Day in Every Way: A Year-Round Calendar of Preschool Learning Challenges provides this kind of thematic curriculum. The weekly themes, chosen for their relevance and interest to preschoolers, help children understand and retain discovered information. A thematic curriculum provides a framework on which children can build new ideas and form generalizations.

The Preschool Program

Checklist of General Goals for Early Childhood Programs

The following goals are essential for a quality early childhood program that builds a sound foundation.

- ❐ Make each child's school experience a positive one.
- ❐ Encourage positive feelings about self, the school, and the environment.
- ❐ Provide opportunities for thinking at all levels: recall, application, analysis, synthesis, and evaluation of knowledge.
- ❐ Stimulate each child's thought processes to bring greater understanding, awareness, and curiosity.
- ❐ Provide an environment and activities that promote optimum physical development.
- ❐ Provide a classroom and program that can meet the needs of each individual child.
- ❐ Encourage sharing and cooperation.
- ❐ Encourage each child to play and work well independently and in groups.
- ❐ Provide opportunities for self-expression for each child through language, dramatics, art, music, and play.
- ❐ Increase each child's attention span.
- ❐ Help each child to recognize the rights, feelings, and property of others.
- ❐ Aid each child to adapt to new situations.
- ❐ Encourage each child to solve problems independently.
- ❐ Foster each child's appreciation for language in many different forms.
- ❐ Introduce the use and need for numbers in daily life.

- ❐ Develop the ability to think logically and make associations.
- ❐ Introduce the concepts of time and order.
- ❐ Increase each child's awareness of the relationship of his or her body and other objects to space.
- ❐ Foster awareness of the environment, our responsibility to it, and the changes that can and do occur in it.
- ❐ Encourage independence in tending to personal needs.
- ❐ Give each child an awareness of the local community and other communities near and far.
- ❐ Encourage safety practices in and out of school. Promote each child's free artistic development and creativity.
- ❐ Provide many different media for creative expression.
- ❐ Foster appreciation for music and the arts. Provide opportunities for exercise individually and in groups.
- ❐ Provide experiences with books, audio-visuals, and other library materials.
- ❐ Foster frequent communication between parents and teachers about each child's overall development.

Checklist for Developing a Preschool Program

Staff

❏ Who will instruct the program? _____
❏ Will there be an aide? _____
❏ What credentials are necessary for the position? _____
_____
❏ Is there a job description? _____
❏ What are the arrangements for substitutes in case of illness or emergency? _____
_____

Students

❏ What population will be served? _____
❏ How many children will be accepted into the program? and of what ages? (Optimum ratios are one adult for every five 3-year-olds, one adult for every eight 4-year-olds, and one adult for every ten 5-year-olds. Day care centers will often increase the number of children per adult to double this amount, and ratios will vary depending on state regulations.) _____
❏ What means will be used to recruit children? _____
_____

Facility

❏ Where will the program be located? _____
❏ Are bathrooms accessible? _____
❏ Is the space adequate for the number of children to be served? (Recommended space is 25 square feet per child.) _____
❏ Is there an outside play area that is safely constructed and fenced, with 75 square feet of play area per child? _____
❏ Is licensing required? _____
❏ Is the facility accessible to the handicapped? _____

Equipment

❏ Are there ample instructional materials for the age group to be served? _____
❏ Has a curriculum been selected? _____
❏ Have all necessary materials and references been ordered? _____
❏ Have parents been notified of supplies and materials that they need to provide? _____
❏ Have community resources (libraries, businesses, churches, second-hand stores) been tapped?
_____

Schedule

❏ Has the schedule been determined? _____
❏ Will children be allowed to attend part of the day every day or only on certain attendance days? _____
❏ Will it be a full-day or part-day program? _____
❏ Will there be child care services in addition to the instructional program? _____

Goals and Objectives

❏ Have parents been oriented about the type of program and its underlying philosophy? _____
❏ What should the parents expect their preschoolers to accomplish? _____

Communication

❏ Have parents received a parent handbook, calendar, and supply list? _____
❏ Have parents completed a background information form? (See pp. 39–44 for sample form.) _____
❏ Have payment procedures been clarified? _____
❏ What type of records will be maintained on each child? (See pp. 47–55 for sample forms.) _____
❏ Will there be written progress reports, conferences, or parent groups? (See pp. 47–55 for sample reports.)

Resources for Every Day in Every Way © 1989

Registration

❑ Have the parents provided records of a physical exam with a health history?_____

❑ Are photo releases needed?_____

❑ Have registration cards been completed? _____

Food Services

❑ Will children bring their own food and snacks, or will the preschool provide food?_____

❑ If the school is responsible for food service, who will prepare the food and at what cost?_____

❑ Are there local health department regulations to be considered? _____

Transportation

❑ How will the children be transported to and from school?_____

❑ Will the preschool offer bus service? _____

❑ Are safety releases necessary? _____

Health and Safety

❑ Are emergency procedures outlined? _____

❑ Are there plans for evacuation and fire drills? _____

❑ How will sick or injured children be treated? _____

Community Relations

❑ Will visitors be allowed?_____

❑ Will there be holiday programs or special functions?_____

❑ Will staff have opportunities to attend community lectures or other educational events?_____

❑ Will there be informational evening meetings?_____

Classroom Learning Centers

An early childhood classroom should be divided into carefully planned learning centers that provide children with a wide range of learning experiences and materials. Learning centers allow young children to choose their own activities and to work and play independently or in small groups at their own pace and ability level.

Although instruction may be teacher directed and structured, during other periods of the day, learning center time should be child directed and open. The teacher may offer group art projects that correlate to the weekly theme, but during center time the easel is always available and the "artist" is free to paint the creation of his or her choice. The teacher may join a small group for a cup of soup, but the "restaurant" is operated by the children.

When arranging learning centers so that children become self-directed in their learning, be sure to allow for smooth traffic flow between centers and for accessibility of materials. Most classrooms use bookshelves and large pieces of equipment to divide the centers. Noisy centers, such as blocks and woodworking, should be spaced away from quieter centers, such as library and investigation. The water table and art center need to be located near the sink.

Often there is a need to limit the number of children allowed in a given center. One helpful technique is to provide a label indicating the number of children a particular center can accommodate. The water table could have six fish pasted on the end of the table, and the block center could have four large squares hanging on the wall.

It is helpful for the educator to keep a checklist to monitor the involvements of each child in the various centers. Though most children will participate in a variety of centers over time, some children may need encouragement to participate in a particular center.

Learning centers give teachers the opportunity to observe and interact with children individually or in small numbers. Much information can be gathered in these centers about each child's interests, peer relationships, and achievements in many different learning areas. Center time offers teachers an opportunity to work with students individually or in small groups on specific skills that may need reinforcement, encouragement, or acceleration. This is the ideal time to listen to a story read by an early reader or to help the child who is interested in learning to tie his shoes.

Set up as many of the following learning centers as your space and resources will allow. If you have limited space, some centers can be rotated throughout the year. The materials in each center should also be rotated. Often equipment will be better used if it is occasionally removed and reintroduced a few weeks later. Too many options in a center can be overwhelming to the young child. Though a child may request a special item to complete an art project, the teacher need not put out every art supply each day. One week the art center may include materials for making fabric collages and fingerpainting, and the following week playdough and watercolor paints could be provided. The colors of tempera paint at the easel can also be varied each day.

Materials in the centers need not be commercial. Junk jewelry, old typewriters, styrofoam packing shells, and tape measures can provide hours of fun for the young child. Parent and community donations should be solicited throughout the year, particularly if the budget is limited.

Large Areas for Whole Group Activities and Active Play

1. Gross Motor Center

Purposes:

- to develop large and small muscle coordination
- to develop balance, posture, locomotion, and strength
- to provide opportunities for group interactions and an outlet for energy

Materials:

- hula hoops
- balance beam
- balls of various sizes and textures
- climbing apparatus
- beanbags
- tricycles, scooters, riding vehicles
- tumbling mat

2. Block Center

Purposes:

- to encourage creativity by taking apart, filling and emptying, sorting and stacking, assembling, and building various constructions
- to promote language, math, fine motor, and coordination skills

Materials:

- large wooden block set
- variety of blocks (plastic, sponge, etc.) of different sizes
- large Duplo and Lego sets
- jumbo dominoes
- small vehicles, animals, and people
- giant Tinkertoys

3. Music Center

Purposes:

- to develop skills of expression, rhythm, listening, and coordination
- to promote understanding and appreciation of music

Materials:

- piano, guitar, or harpsichord
- rhythm instruments
- record player and records
- cassette player and tapes

4. Group Gathering Center

Purpose:

- to offer opportunities for large-group activities such as storytime and circle time
- during center time children often bring materials from the block or music centers, play a group game, or perform a motor activity

Materials:

- rug or carpeting
- large bulletin board
- flannelboard
- blackboard and chalk
- chart rack for writing experience stories
- charts with words to rhymes and fingerplays
- calendar, birthday boards, weather charts
- filmstrip projector and filmstrips

Imagination Areas

1. Housekeeping Center

Purposes:

- to encourage dramatic play, social interaction, and self-expression
- to stimulate language and discourse skills

Materials:

- small table and chairs
- kitchen appliances (stove, fridge, sink, etc.)
- toy dishes, pots and pans, and utensils
- artificial or plastic food
- dolls and clothing
- doll equipment, such as beds, strollers, and high chair
- cash register with play money, bags, stamps, boxes
- shopping cart
- ironing board, iron
- cleaning equipment, such as brooms, mops, and feather dusters
- telephones

2. Drama and Dress-up Center

Purposes:

- to encourage role-playing
- to build self-confidence and self-esteem
- to provide practice in dressing and undressing skills
- to develop language and expressive skills

Materials:

- puppets
- puppet stage
- masks
- costumes, such as Superman, animals, princess
- hats, such as firefighter, cowboy, lady, police officer
- clothing, including shirts, dresses, shoes, pants, boots
- accessories, including scarves, jewelry, purses, wallets, suitcases
- full-length mirror
- toy camera

3. Art Center

Purposes:

- to encourage individual expression and creativity
- to offer opportunities to explore a variety of media in a variety of ways
- to develop a sense of personal accomplishment
- to enhance fine and visual perception skills

Materials:

- painting easels
- drying rack
- work tables
- bulletin board to display work
- various paints: fingerpaints, tempera, water colors
- painting materials: brushes, rollers, paper
- various colors, textures, and sizes of paper
- scissors (easy-grip, lefties, and standard)
- writing apparatus, such as pencils, crayons, markers, chalk
- clay, playdough, and clay tools
- glue, paste, and tape
- craft materials, such as paper, wallpaper, and fabric scraps
- sponges, pipe cleaners, toothpicks, cotton swabs, wood sticks
- cookie cutters, rolling pins, utensils
- stapler, paper punch, paper clips, rulers
- yarn, string, rope, and ribbon
- cotton balls, colored tissues, paper towels
- rubber stamps and stamp pads
- junk items, such as bottle tops, shells, beans, and styrofoam

Sensory Exploration Areas

1. Sand-Water Table Center

Purposes:

- to provide tactile-sensory stimulation
- to help children use their senses for investigation
- to develop problem-solving skills
- to promote verbal expression, socialization, and emotional relaxation

Materials:

- water, sand, or a combination sand-and-water table
- plastic aprons
- pans, shovels, buckets, sieves, funnels, tubes
- sink and float objects
- egg beater
- boats

2. Woodworking Center

(To insure that safety procedures are adhered to, this center should operate under direct adult supervision.)

Purposes:

- to promote cooperation and respect for property and safety rules
- to encourage skills of expression, eye-hand coordination, and number relations

Materials:

- hammers, wrenches, screwdrivers, pliers, and saws
- nails, glue, screws, tacks
- wood, cork, styrofoam, and other construction materials
- vise
- work table

3. Investigation Center

Often the educator is on hand to encourage problem solving with various science experiments that are set up through the school year.

Purpose:

- to stimulate cognitive development by encouraging children to reason, analyze, explore, and classify

Materials:

- color wheels
- magnets and magnetic objects
- tape measures and measuring cups
- balance scales
- prisms
- magnifying glasses
- kaleidoscopes
- live animals
- plants and nature exhibits
- rocks, shells, beans, and other objects to classify
- mystery and "feely" boxes
- tactile textures
- sounds and smells containers
- egg timer and clocks

Quiet Activity Areas

1. Library Center

Purposes:

- to promote language and reading readiness skills
- to develop an appreciation for literature

Materials:

- cozy seating area (pillows, sofa, rocker, or beanbag chairs)
- stuffed animals
- set of books and a rotating selection from the library
- tape recorder with earphones
- cassette-book sets for reading independently
- storytelling pictures
- display racks and bookshelves

2. Fine Motor Center

Purposes:

- to develop eye-hand coordination and visual perception skills
- to enhance problem solving, classification, and discrimination skills

Materials:

- crayons, pencils, and markers
- various sizes, colors, and types of paper

- sandpaper shapes, letters, and numbers
- stencils, templates, and rulers
- primary typewriter
- stapler and hole puncher
- small chalkboard and chalk
- desk or work table
- puzzles of graduated levels of difficulty
- pegboards and pegs of various sizes
- Lego sets
- parquetry designs
- small building blocks
- lacing and sewing cards
- stringing beads of various sizes and shapes
- tactile letter and number boards

3. Individual Instruction Center

Purposes:

- for teacher to work with individual children or small groups to reinforce specific concepts or provide individually targeted challenges
- for children to work independently with materials that will enhance cognitive skills

Materials:

- computer
- board games, such as Chutes and Ladders and Candyland
- electronic games
- dominoes
- abacuses
- math manipulatives
- feltboard shapes, numbers, letters, and objects
- matching games, such as Lotto, Bingo, and Memory
- sequence cards and puzzles
- rhyming cards
- spatial relationship cards
- picture cards and category cards
- what's-missing puzzles and picture cards

Special Interest Center

Purpose:

- a temporary interest center with materials and activities that relate to the weekly theme (this center can be established separately or incorporated into existing centers)

Ideas:

- additional costumes in drama center for Halloween
- a post office during Valentine's Day week
- restaurant
- doctor's office
- grocery store
- hairdresser's salon
- shoeshine stand
- Santa's Workshop
- bakery
- greenhouse
- ice cream parlor
- circus ring
- launching pad
- laundromat
- hospital nursery
- a beach with sand, umbrella, and towel
- a camping tent
- train
- hardware store or workshop

Diagnostic Instruments for Young Children

Testing, particularly of young children and of children from different ethnic backgrounds, is controversial, and many evaluative instruments on the market are of poor quality. Despite these drawbacks, the assessment of children in early childhood programs can provide valuable information to help meet individual needs and to improve program quality.

Basically, assessment in the early childhood program is for the following purposes:

- **Screening**, or sampling children's behavior in various areas in order to identify those who may need further diagnostic evaluations;
- **Diagnosis**, or determining through in-depth evaluation if a child has a special need and if specialized services are warranted;
- **Program planning**, or improving the quality of the curriculum by considering individual children's strengths and weakness; and
- **Program evaluation**, or assessing whether the goals of the program are being met and the instruction has been effective.

Evaluation must be ongoing, and programs should be continually assessed by informal methods. Formal instruments should be used only at specified times, and they must be properly administered, scored, and interpreted. It is important to look at the child's performance, not merely at the test score, and to interpret the information in the context of the curriculum and the child's background.

If you use a diagnostic instrument, be sure that it is appropriate for the type of program and for the children. In addition, you should take personal and environmental variables into consideration to provide uniformity for each participant. Most important, however, seek the appropriate assistance and training to ensure that all assessments are properly conducted.

Vision and hearing screenings, as well as a general physical examination accompanied by a health history, are standard supplements to the general screening program for young children. Often a speech and language therapist conducts a speech and language screening at the time of the preschool screening.

There are numerous diagnostic instruments for young children currently on the market. Test anthologies, such as *Mental Measurements Yearbook,* can be found in most university libraries and contain critical reviews by authorities for the majority of available tests. The following assessments have been previewed by the authors and are considered suitable for administration by a trained early childhood educator.

ABC Inventory to Determine Kindergarten and School Readiness

By Norman Adair and George Blesch. Research Concepts, A Division of Test Maker, Inc., 1368 East Airport Road, Muskegon, MI 49444. 1985.
Purpose: To identify children who do not have the readiness skills that will enable them to master prereading skills in kindergarten and first grade. The child draws a man, answers questions about characteristics of objects and general topics, and performs tasks involving numbers and shapes.
Administration: This individually administered test takes 10–15 minutes to give and score. It is designed for children between the ages of 4 and 7.

Basic School Skills Inventory

By Libby Goodman and Donald Hammill. Follett Publishing Company, 1010 West Washington Boulevard, Chicago, IL 60607. 1975.
Purpose: To identify learning difficulties in children in the developmental age range of 4 to 6 years. The instrument assesses seven areas of school performance identified by classroom teachers as being important to academic success. There are 84 items representing the following areas of school performance: basic communication, handwriting, oral communication, self-help, reading readiness, number readiness, and classroom behavior.
Administration: This individually administered test takes about 20 minutes to give. It is designed for children between the developmental ages of 4 and 6.

Battelle Developmental Inventory

By Jean Newborg, John Stock, Linda Wnek, John Guidubaldi, and John Svinicki. DLM Teaching Resources, One DLM Park, Allen, TX 75002. 1984.
Purpose: To identify children who are handicapped or delayed in several areas of development. Includes a screening test and full battery. The following domains are assessed: personal-social, adaptive, motor, communica-tion, and cognitive.
Administration: Individually administered, the screening test takes 10–30 minutes and the full battery takes 60–90 minutes. The tests are designed for children from birth to 8 years.

Boehm Test of Basic Concepts—Preschool Version

By Anne E. Boehm. Psychological Corporation, 555 Academic Court, San Antonio, TX 78204-2498. 1986.
Purpose: To measure understanding of 26 basic relational concepts that help children understand and describe the world around them. A picture test consisting of 52 items.
Administration: Individually administered in 10 to 15 minutes. It is designed for 3- to 5-year-old children or older children with identified language difficulties.

Boehm Test of Basic Concepts, Revised

By Anne E. Boehm. Psychological Corporation, 555 Academic Court, San Antonio, TX 78204-2498. 1986.
Purpose: To measure mastery of basic concepts generally considered important for complying with teacher verbal instructions and for achievement during the first years of school. A picture test measuring 50 concepts singly and in combination.
Administration: Group-administered in 30 minutes; can also be administered individually. It is designed for kindergarten through second-grade children.

Bilingual Syntax Measure

By Marina K. Burt, Heidi C. Duley, and Eduardo Hernandez. Harcourt Brace Jovanovich, 757 Third Avenue, New York, NY 10017. 1975.
Purpose: To measure children's oral proficiency in English or Spanish grammatical structures by using natural speech as a basis for making judgments. Measures five levels of language proficiency from level 1 (the child neither speaks nor comprehends the language in which the test is being administered) to level 5 (the child is as proficient as peers who are

native speakers of that language). Also indicates to the teacher the child's strengths and weaknesses in the basic structures of either or both languages.

Administration: The BSM is individually administered and takes 10–15 minutes to give. It is designed primarily for children between 4 and 9 years of age.

Bracken Basic Concept Scale

By Bruce A. Bracken. Charles Merrill, A Division of Bell and Howell, 936 Eastwind Drive, Westerville, OH 43081. 1984.

Purpose: To assess an individual child's conceptual knowledge by measuring 258 concepts in the following categories: colors, letter identification, numbers and counting, comparisons, shapes, direction and position, social and emotional, size, texture and material, quantity, and time and sequence. Can be used as a diagnostic or a screening measure.

Administration: This test is individually administered and takes 5–10 minutes for screening and 30–35 minutes for the diagnostic scale. It is designed to screen children between the ages of 5 and 7 and as a diagnostic measure for children between the ages of 2 years 6 months and 7 years 11 months.

Brigance K and 1 Screen

By Albert H. Brigance. Curriculum Associates, Inc., 5 Esquire Road, North Billerica, MA 01862-2589. 1982.

Purpose: To provide a quick screening that obtains a broad sampling of a student's skills and behaviors. Can identify students warranting a more comprehensive evaluation as well as assist in program planning and pupil groupings.

Administration: Can be administered individually in about 10–12 minutes per child, or by a team of four staff members. It is designed to screen children from 4 years 9 months to 7 years. It is often administered before the end of the school year or just before the opening of school in September. It may be used throughout the year to determine placements and individual student plans.

Brigance Preschool Screen for Three- and Four-Year-Olds

By Albert H. Brigance. Curriculum Associates, Inc., 5 Esquire Road, North Billerica, MA 01862-2589. 1985.

Purpose: To obtain a sampling of the 3- and 4-year-old child's skills and behaviors in order to identify the child who should be referred for more comprehensive evaluation. Eight supplemental assessments can also be used to help indicate gifted students. Can assist in program planning and determining appropriate student placements. The data sheet of results is criterion- and curriculum-referenced so that data can be translated into instructional objectives.

Administration: The screening can be administered individually in 10–12 minutes and assesses a variety of areas. Separate tests are provided for the age groups 2 years 6 months to 3 years and 3 years 1 month to 5 years.

Burks' Behavior Rating Scales (Preschool and Kindergarten Edition)

By Harold F. Burks. Western Psychological Services, 12031 Wilshire Boulevard, Los Angeles, CA 90025. 1977.

Purpose: To attempt to gauge the severity of negative symptoms noted by educators and parents by rating specific behaviors observed in the young child. The information gathered can be used to determine if additional evaluation is warranted or to help identify goals and objectives appropriate for an individual child. The manual offers possible intervention approaches that focus on facilitating adult change in order to ultimately achieve change in the behavior of the child. The 18 subscales measure behavior such as poor attention, excessive anxiety, and poor anger control.

Administration: Because raters judge each of the 18 behaviors described in the assessment according to a five-point scale based on frequency of behavior observed over a period of time, it is helpful to have more than one person who is knowledgeable about the child's daily behavior complete the survey. This instrument is designed for children between the ages of 3 through 6.

Denver Developmental Screening Test

By William K. Frankenburg and Josiah B. Dodds. Ladoca Project and Publishing Foundation, East 51st Avenue and Lincoln Street, Denver, CO 80216. 1973.

Purpose: A simple, useful standardized tool to aid in the early identification of children with developmental problems. The DDST screens children in the following areas: personal-social, fine motor–adaptive, gross motor, and language.

Administration: This individually administered screening instrument takes 15–20 minutes. It is designed for children from 2 weeks through 6 years of age.

Developmental Indicators for the Assessment of Learning, Revised Edition (DIAL-R)

By Carol D. Mardell-Czudnowski and Dorothy Goldberg. Childcraft Education Corporation, 20 Kilmer Road, Edison, NJ 08818. 1983.

Purpose: A screening instrument to assist in the identification of children who may have special education needs. This assessment can also be used to help identify students' strengths and weaknesses as a tool for curriculum and program development. The DIAL assesses motor, concept, and language functions.

Administration: This test is given by a team, usually led by a professional and composed of paraprofessionals or trained volunteers, and it takes about 25 minutes to assess each child. It is designed for children from 2 to 6 years of age.

The Developmental Profile

By Gerald Alpern and Thomas Boll. Psychological Development Publications, P.O. Box 3196, Aspen, CO 81611. 1972.

Purpose: To assess a child's development from birth to preadolescence as a quick general screen and to assist in the general development of individual curriculum prescriptions. This profile consists of 217 items arranged into five scales, which are divided by age levels, and it gives a broad picture of a child's functioning.

Administration: This scale, which should be administered by someone who knows the child well, takes about 20–40 minutes to give. It is designed for children from birth to 12 years of age.

Diagnostic Inventory of Early Development

By Albert H. Brigance. Curriculum Associates, 5 Esquire Road, North Billerica, MA 01862-2589. 1978.

Purpose: To simplify and combine the processes of assessing, diagnosing, record keeping, and instructional planning for young children. A color-coded record-keeping system is used to identify skills mastered and objectives identified by each evaluation, thus providing an ongoing record of the child's performance. Skill sequences are monitored for the following areas: psychomotor, self-help, speech and language, general knowledge and comprehension, and early academic skills.

Administration: The testing time for this individually administered inventory varies with the methods used and with the characteristics of each child. It is designed for children from infancy through the developmental age of 7.

Fluharty Preschool Speech and Language Screening Test

By Nancy Buona Fluharty. DLM Teaching Resources, P.O. Box 4000, One DLM Park, Allen, TX 75002. 1978.

Purpose: To measure early speech and language performance to identify children in need of in-depth diagnostic evaluation of speech and language skills.

Administration: This screening test is individually administered in 5–10 minutes. It tests syntax, auditory comprehension, and target identification of articulation in children ages 2 to 6.

The Metropolitan Readiness Test, Level K-1

By Joanne R. Nurss and Mary E. McGauvran. Psychological Corporation, 555 Academic Court, San Antonio, TX 78204-2498. 1976.
Purpose: To assess kindergarten-age children's readiness for school-related tasks. It contains 7 subtests and yields percentile and stanine scores for visual and language skills and presents a composite prereading score.
Administration: This group test is administered in different sittings to kindergarten-age children.

Peabody Picture Vocabulary Test PPVT-R)

By Lloyd M. Dunn and Leota M. Dunn. American Guidance Service, Publisher's Building, Circle Pines, MN 55014. 1981.
Purpose: Primarily to measure the child's receptive vocabulary for Standard American English by choosing a picture that best defines the word said by the examiner from a plate of four pictures.
Administration: Often used by speech and language therapists, the PPVT can also be administered by the early childhood educator with proper training in about 10–20 minutes. The test is designed for children from 2 years 6 months through adults.

Portage Guide to Early Education

By the Portage Project. Cooperative Education Service Agency #5, 626 East Slifer Street, Portage, WI 53901. 1976.
Purpose: To guide those who need to assess the behavior of young children and to plan realistic curriculum goals. There is a checklist and card file of possible teaching methods that aid in the assessing of present behavior, targeting of emerging behavior, and determining of techniques to teach specific behaviors. The checklist is color-coded and divided into the following ideas: infant stimulation, socialization, language, self-help, cognition, and motor.

Administration: For children between the mental ages of birth and six years of age. A checklist is usually individually administered to a child upon entry, and behaviors are monitored throughout the school year with the checklist serving as an ongoing curriculum record.

School Readiness Checklist, Revised Edition

By John J. Austin and J. Clayton Lafferty. Research Concepts, A Division of Test Maker, Inc., 1368 East Airport Road, Muskegon, MI 49444. 1987.
Purpose: To assist in appraising a young child's readiness for school. This scale of 43 questions is intended to aid in determining readiness for standard kindergarten.
Administration: Designed for use by parents, this checklist is also appropriate for use by early childhood teachers. Parent fills out questionnaire and derives a score that indicates the child's approximate state of readiness for school. Estimated completion time is 15 minutes.

Test of Verbal and Nonverbal Language Functioning

By Elaine P. Hannah and Julie O. Gardner. Lingua Press, P.O. Box 293, Northridge, CA 91324. 1978.
Purpose: To screen English- and Spanish-speaking preschool children. Because this assessment has a separate nonverbal core, it is useful for the child with little or no expressive language ability. Its scales include visual perception, conceptual development, auditory perception, and linguistic development. Each has a percentile score.
Administration: In this individually administered test, the child indicates understanding of directions and concepts through manipulation of objects and picture cards. It is designed for children from 3 years 6 months to 5 years 6 months.

A free preschool eye chart to detect vision problems is offered by the National Society to Prevent Blindness, 500 E. Remington Road, Dept. FC, Schaumburg, IL 60173.

Early Warning Signs of Special Needs

Share the following checklist with parents, so they can assist in the early identification of preschoolers with special needs. Remind parents that these are warning signs, not definite indications that a problem currently exists. If there is concern about a preschool child's development, consult the local school district or education agency.

The following checklist is derived from a pamphlet distributed by the Loess Hills Area Education Agency XIII, Council Bluffs, Iowa.

Does Your Child Have Special Needs?

The following items are warning signs that problems may develop; they do not necessarily mean that problems are already present. If you check any of the following items, consult your doctor or the local school district or education agency.

Seeing

If the child
- ❑ does not look at toys or people and try to reach for them
- ❑ frequently rubs his or her eyes
- ❑ has red, watering, or encrusted eyes
- ❑ sometimes or always crosses one or both eyes
- ❑ does not notice distant objects

Hearing

If the child
- ❑ does not startle at loud noises
- ❑ does not turn to face sounds and noises by 6 months
- ❑ has frequent earaches, running ears, or running nose
- ❑ does not understand spoken conversation or directions
- ❑ talks in an unusually low voice

Talking

If the child
- ❑ does not babble and coo as an infant
- ❑ cannot say the names of a few people and toys by age 2
- ❑ cannot tell you about two things that happened to him or her by age 3
- ❑ does not talk in short sentences by age 4

Moving

If the child
- ❑ is unable to sit by age 1
- ❑ is unable to walk by age 2
- ❑ is unable to throw and kick a ball by age 3
- ❑ is unable to run by age 4
- ❑ is unable to hop on one foot by age 5

Thinking

If the child
- ❑ does not respond to his or her name by age 1
- ❑ does not point to eyes, ears, nose, and mouth by age 2
- ❑ does not know "big" and "little" by age 3
- ❑ does not know three colors by age 4
- ❑ does not count to five by age 5

Helping

If the child
- ❑ has trouble sucking a bottle as a newborn
- ❑ does not use a spoon by age 2
- ❑ is not out of diapers by age 3
- ❑ does not play cooperatively with other children by age 4
- ❑ cannot dress himself or herself by age 5

Parents:

This list of early warning signs will help you know if a problem might develop. If you think your child may have special needs, seek help now. Fortunately, many developmental delays and handicapping conditions can be helped or completely corrected if parents recognize the problem early and seek help.

Resources for Every Day in Every Way © 1989

Background Information Form for Preschool Students

Child's Name _____ Birthdate _____

Sex _____ Place of Birth _____ Nationality _____

Address _____ Telephone _____

Name of Mother or Guardian _____ Age _____

Occupation _____ Work Phone _____

Name of Father or Guardian _____ Age _____

Occupation _____ Work Phone _____

Marital Status of Parents _____

Custody-Visiting Arrangements _____

If child is adopted, list age at adoption _____

Is child aware of adoption? _____

List siblings and their ages _____

_____

_____

_____

Are there other members of the household? If so, list name, age, and relationship _____

_____

Is your child toilet trained? _____ Describe assistance needed

and words used _____

Does your child nap? _____ When? _____

What time does your child go to bed at night? _____ Wake up? _____

Does your child have any special fears? _____

Does your child have any problems with vision or hearing? _____

If so, please explain _____

_____

Does your child have any health problems that we should be aware of? _____

Please explain _____

_____

_____

Are there any foods or drinks that your child should not have? _____
_____

What does your child usually eat for breakfast? _____

Do you have any concerns about any aspect of your child's development? _____
_____
_____

Age at which your child...

Crawled on hands and knees _____ Sat alone _____ Walked _____
Named simple objects _____ Spoke in complete sentences _____
Slept through the night _____ Toilet trained _____
Do you feel your child's speech is clear? _____ Can strangers understand
when he or she speaks? _____

Is any language other than English used in the home? If so, please describe _____
_____
_____

List illnesses your child has had _____
Does your child have frequent colds? _____ Earaches? _____
Sore throats? _____ Stomachaches? _____ Fevers? _____
Has your child had any serious accidents or operations? _____
If so, please describe _____
_____
_____

Does your child have any allergies? _____
If so, please describe _____
Does your child take any regular medication? _____
When was your child last to a doctor? _____ Dentist? _____
Are there any special medical, physical, or emotional needs that the school or staff should be
aware of? _____
_____
_____

How much television does your child generally watch each day? _____
_____

What are your child's favorite activities? _____
_____

What does your child enjoy doing with mother? _____
_____

What does your child enjoy doing with father? _____

Does your child play well alone? _____ In groups? _____
Are there neighborhood playmates? _____ If so, with what age children
does your child usually play? _____
Does your child accept correction easily? _____
What is the method of behavior control used in your home? _____
_____

Please circle items below that describe your child . . .

Happy	Aggressive	Friendly	Moody	Clumsy
Dependent	Stubborn	Impulsive	Fearful	Quiet
Good-natured	Even-tempered	Attentive	Sympathetic	Shy
Sleepy				

Other: _____

Has your child learned to . . .

Say nursery rhymes? _____ Sing songs? _____
Listen to stories? _____ Say his or her name? _____
State his or her age and sex? _____ Dress self independently? _
Recognize and name common objects? _____
Count? _____ How far? _____
Follow simple directions? _____ Throw and catch a ball? ____
Name basic colors? _____ Hop on one foot? _____
Balance on one foot? _____ Ride a tricycle? _____
Write name? _____ Draw a person? _____
Other? (Please note additional significant accomplishments) _____

Has your child had group play experience? _____
Has your child been cared for by someone besides the family? _____
If so, please describe _____
_____

Has your child gone to preschool or daycare before? _____
Please describe previous experiences _____
_____
_____
_____

What do you hope will be included in your child's preschool program? _____
_____
_____
_____
_____

Emergency Information

Persons Authorized to Pick Up Your Child:

Name _____ Relationship _____

Name _____ Relationship _____

Name _____ Relationship _____

Name _____ Relationship _____

Persons to Be Notified in Case of Emergency:

Name _____ Phone _____

Name _____ Phone _____

Name _____ Phone _____

Child's Physician _____ Phone _____

Address _____

Emergency Hospital Preference _____

_____   _____
Date   Parent Signature

For Staff Reference: Check those on file:

Immunization Record _____ Physical Examination _____ Birth Certificate _____

Resources for Every Day in Every Way © 1989

Progress Reports for Preschool and Kindergarten

Progress reports are important because they not only help you evaluate the effectiveness of instruction, but they also facilitate parent-teacher communication. In addition to scheduled report cards and notes sent home throughout the year, parent-teacher conferences are essential to a good early childhood education program because parent-teacher communication should be ongoing.

The following samples of kindergarten and prekindergarten progress reports and a parent-teacher conference form provide guidelines for effectively communicating with parents.

Kindergarten Student Progress Report

Name _____   **Class** _____

Teacher _____   **Year** _____

A Note to Parents

The purpose of this report card is to inform you of your child's progress in school. We believe that each child has a different level of maturity and abilities. Understanding and encouragement are the most positive attitudes that parents can take when discussing this progress report with their child.

The marks **A** for **Almost Always**, **S** for **Sometimes**, and **N** for **Not Yet** are based on each child's maturity level and ability. Empty blocks mean the activity has not been introduced.

Feel free to contact the teacher about any questions you might have. Please sign and return the card to the teacher.

Parent's Signature

1st marking period

_____   **Date** _____

2nd marking period

_____   **Date** _____

3rd marking period

_____   **Date** _____

4th marking period

_____   **Date** _____

Attendance
Days Absent
1st marking period
_____
2nd marking period
_____
3rd marking period
_____
4th marking period
_____

Resources for Every Day in Every Way © 1989

Work Habits and Social-Emotional Skills

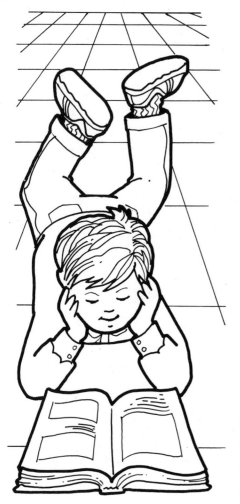

	1	2	3	4
Listens				
Participates in group discussions				
Completes assigned tasks				
Works independently				
Exhibits self-control				
Respects rights and property of others				
Shares and plays cooperatively				
Assumes responsibility				
Is courteous				
Distinguishes reality from fantasy.				

Language Arts Skills

	1	2	3	4
Recognizes and writes name				
Says the alphabet				
Recognizes the letters studied				
Says the sounds for the letters studied				
Writes the letters introduced				
Distinguishes words that rhyme				
Retells a story in proper sequence				
Listens to stories and poems with interest				
Uses and enjoys library privileges				
Creates stories from imagination				
Has correct pencil grasp				
Demonstrates left to right progression				

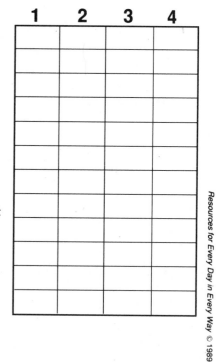

Mathematics

	1	2	3	4
Matches sets from zero to ten				
Associates numerals with corresponding group				
Distinguishes sets of more, less, and equal				
Counts to ten				
Counts to twenty				
Writes numerals to ten				
Uses ordinal numerals, first to fifth				
Identifies simple shapes				
Recognizes differences in size and shape				
Classifies objects				
Identifies patterns				

Social Studies and Science

	1	2	3	4
Participates in discussions and activities				
Understands concepts taught				
Shows ability to work independently and with a group				
Demonstrates problem-solving abilities				

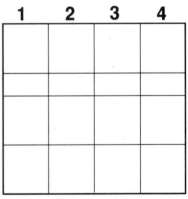

Health and Safety

	1	2	3	4
Appears to be well rested				
Dresses himself or herself				
Shows large motor coordination				
Shows fine motor coordination (cutting, painting, etc.)				
Knows address				
Knows telephone number				

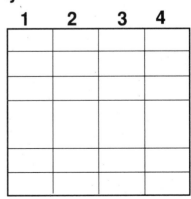

Special Subjects

Art

Understands art concepts taught

Is able to use various media

Listens to instructions and follows
directions

1	2	3	4

Music

Participates in musical activities

Understands music concepts taught

1	2	3	4

Physical Education

Is able to perform basic motor skills

Listens to instructions and follows
directions

Works well with others

1	2	3	4

Comments

1st marking period _____

_____

_____

_____

2nd marking period _____

_____

_____

3rd marking period _____

_____

_____

_____

4th marking period _____

_____

_____

_____

(ADAPTED FROM THE AMERICAN SCHOOL OF MADRID KINDERGARTEN PROGRESS REPORT)

Prekindergarten Student Progress Report

NAME _____ **TEACHER** _____

BIRTH DATE _____ **YEAR** _____

The purpose of this report is to provide the parent of prekindergarten students with information regarding their child's progress. The children are introduced to many skills in prekindergarten, and prekindergarten students grow and develop rapidly. Each child has an individual rate of development, and there will be a large range in the developmental levels of these young children. Anytime a parent has a special concern about his or her child's progress, a parent-teacher conference should be requested.

GRADING KEY		
A	-	Almost Always
E	-	Emerging
N	-	Needs Attention

PARENT SIGNATURE

PLEASE REVIEW, SIGN, AND RETURN TO SCHOOL.

1st marking period _____ 2nd marking period _____

Date _____ Date _____

3rd marking period _____ 4th marking period _____

Date _____ Date _____

I take care of my personal needs

I relax and rest at nap time

I care for toys and school materials

I show fine visual-motor coordination

I show gross motor coordination

I march and move to music

I participate in group activities

I can work independently

READING MATH

I use the learning center consistently

I listen and follow directions

My name is Anna, What is your name?

I speak in complete sentences

We went to the zoo yesterday.

I use acceptable grammar and pronunciation

I follow school rules and procedures

I share and play cooperatively

I indicate positive feelings about myself

I sing familiar songs and rhymes

I use tools and materials for construction

I draw, paint, and color pictures

I use outdoor play equipment

I am interested in stories and books

I am curious about my environment

I can associate related items

I can classify and categorize sets

I learn concepts presented

LANGUAGE ABILITY:

    Comments: _____

_____

_____

HAND PREFERENCE:

    Comments: _____

_____

_____

VISION, HEARING, HEALTH NEEDS:

    Comments: _____

_____

_____

SPECIAL ABILITIES OR TALENTS: _____

_____

_____

SPECIAL CONCERNS: _____

_____

_____

SPECIAL SERVICES PROVIDED: _____

_____

_____

ADDITIONAL COMMENTS: _____

_____

_____

_____

_____

_____

_____

Resources for Every Day in Every Way © 1989

(ADAPTED FROM THE AMERICAN SCHOOL OF MADRID PREKINDERGARTEN PROGRESS REPORT)

Parent-Teacher Conference Form

Person conducting conference _____   Date _____

Parent(s) present _____   Others present _____

Reason for conference _____

Child's Name _____   Birth date _____

Age _____   Class _____

Language Development: _____

Cognitive Development: _____

Motor Development: _____

Social-Emotional Development: _____

Child's favorite activities _____

Special achievements _____

Special concerns _____

Parent comments _____

Summary of conference _____

_____

_____

_____

_____

_____

Songs, Rhymes, and Fingerplays

The following collection includes over 225 new and traditional songs, rhymes, and fingerplays. All have been tested with young children, who reacted with great enthusiasm.

Many of the fingerplays can easily be used with a flannelboard and are starred (✳).

ABC Song (Traditional)

A, B, C, D, E, F, G,
H, I, J, K, L, M, N, O, P,
Q, R, S, T, U, V,
W, X, Y, AND Z.
Now I know my ABCs.
Next time won't you sing with me?

A-hunting We Will Go (Traditional)

A-hunting we will go,
A-hunting we will go.
We'll catch a fox,
And put him in a box,
And then we'll let him go.

Aiken Drum (Traditional-Scottish)

Chorus:
There was a man lived in the moon,
In the moon, in the moon.
There was a man lived in the moon,
And his name was Aiken Drum.
And he played upon a ladle,
A ladle, a ladle,
And he played upon a ladle,
And his name was Aiken Drum.

His hair was made of green cheese,
Of green cheese, of green cheese.
His hair was made of green cheese,
And his name was Aiken Drum.

His eyes were made of meatballs . . .

His coat was made of pizza . . .

His shoes were made of peanuts . . .

His pants were made of *(children make up)* . . .

His hat was made of *(children make up)* . . .

(Repeat chorus)

Airplane (Cynthia Holley)

I am a big airplane,
With wings so wide and strong.
(Hold arms out like wings.)
My tail stands straight up in the air,
And my body's very long.
*(Stand on one foot, stretching one leg behind,
  extended in air.)*
Watch me when I'm flying,
For I go very fast.
*(Standing on foot, move extended arms in
  flying motion.)*
Let's see who can stay up in the air,
And who runs out of gas!
(Children remain balanced on one foot.)

America the Beautiful (Katharine Lee Bates)

O beautiful for spacious skies, for amber
  waves of grain,
For purple mountain majesties above the
  fruited plain.
America! America! God shed His grace on
  thee,
And crown thy good with brotherhood from sea
  to shining sea.

The Animal Fair (Traditional)

I went to the animal fair.
The animals all were there.
The old baboon by the light of the moon
Was combing his auburn hair.
The monkey sure was spunk.
He climbed up the elephant's trunk.
The elephant sneezed and fell to his knees,
And that was the end of the monk, monk,
  monk, monk!

Animal Poem (Traditional)

We'll hop, hop, hop like a bunny,
*(With two fingers in the air, imitate hopping with
  hands.)*
We'll run, run, run like a dog,
(Wiggle fingers to imitate running.)
We'll swim, swim, swim like a turtle,
(Move hands in swimming motion.)
And we'll jump, jump, jump like a frog,
*(Two fingers jump and jump in palm of opposite
  hand.)*
We'll tromp, tromp, tromp like an elephant,
(Move hands up and down heavily.)
We'll fly, fly, fly like a bird,
(Wave arms in flying motion.)
Then we'll sit right down and fold our hands
(Sit down and fold hands in lap.)
And not say a single word.

The Ants Go Marching (Traditional)

The ants go marching one by one. Hoorah, hoorah!
The ants go marching one by one. Hoorah, hoorah!
The ants go marching one by one,
And the little one stops to shoot a gun.
And they all keep marching down to the earth
To get out of the rain.
BOOM, BOOM, BOOM, BOOM, BOOM-BOOM-BOOM, BOOM.

The ants go marching two by two. Hoorah, hoorah!
The ants go marching two by two. Hoorah, hoorah!
The ants go marching two by two,
And the little one stops to tie his shoe.
And they all keep marching down to the earth
To get out of the rain.
BOOM, BOOM, BOOM, BOOM, BOOM-BOOM-BOOM, BOOM.

. . . The ants go marching three by three,
And the little one stops to climb a tree. . .

. . . The ants go marching four by four,
And the little one stops to shut the door. . .

. . . The ants go marching five by five,
And the little one stops to sing and jive. . .

. . . The ants go marching six by six,
And the little one stops to pick up sticks. . .

. . . The ants go marching seven by seven,
And the little one stops and looks to heaven. . .

. . . The ants go marching eight by eight,
And the little one stops to open the gate. . .

. . . The ants go marching nine by nine,
And the little one stops to scratch his spine. . .

. . . The ants go marching ten by ten,
And the little one stops to pet a hen,
And they all keep marching down to the earth
To get out of the rain.
BOOM . . .

(Imitate designated movements.)

Apple Tree (Traditional)

Way up high in an apple tree,
Two little apples smiled at me.
(Point up in air, smile, and touch lips.)
I shook that tree as hard as I could,
(Imitate shaking tree.)
Down came those apples,
Mmmmmmm, they were good.
(Make motion with arms of falling apples, rub tummy.)

A-tisket, A-tasket (Traditional)

A-tisket, a-tasket, a green and yellow basket.
I wrote a letter to my friend, and on the way I lost it,
I lost it, I lost it, and on the way I lost it.
A little boy picked it up and put it in his pocket!

(This can be played as a game. Children stand in circle and one child skips around outside of circle, dropping a letter behind a child. This child chases "it" around the circle.)

August Heat (Anonymous)

In August, when the days are hot,
I like to find a shady spot,
And hardly move a single bit—
And sit—
And sit—
And sit—
And sit!

Baa, Baa, Black Sheep (Nursery Rhyme)

Baa, baa, black sheep, have you any wool?
Yes sir, yes sir, three bags full.
One for my master and one for my dame
And one for the little boy that lives down the lane.

Baby Bumblebee (Traditional)

I'm bringing home a baby bumblebee.
Won't my mommy be so proud of me?
I'm bringing home a baby bumblebee.
OUCH! ! ! He bit me!

(Hold fist closed and swing arm back and forth. Open fist for "OUCH.")

Baby Grows (Traditional)

Five little fingers on this hand,
(Hold up one hand.)
Five little fingers on that,
(Hold up the other hand.)
A dear little nose,
(Point to nose.)
A mouth like a rose,
(Point to mouth.)
Two cheeks so tiny and fat.
(Point to both cheeks.)
Two eyes and two ears
(Point to both eyes and ears.)
And ten little toes,
(Point to toes.)
That is the way the baby grows!

Baby's Toys (Adapted)*

Here's a ball for baby, big and soft and round.
(Make a circle with thumbs and index fingers.)
Here is baby's hammer, oh, how he (she) can
  pound!
(Pound one fist on the other.)
Here is baby's music—clapping, clapping so!
(Clap hands.)
Here are baby's dollies, standing in a row.
(Hold up ten fingers.)
Here is baby's trumpet—toot-toot-too!
(Imitate playing trumpet with hands.)
Here's the way the baby plays peek-a-boo.
(Cover face and open fingers to peek out.)
Here's a big umbrella to keep baby dry.
(Hold hands up, forming umbrella.)
Here's the way baby goes a-lullabye.
(Make rocking motion with hands.)

The Bear Went Over the Mountain
(Traditional)

The bear went over the mountain,
The bear went over the mountain,
The bear went over the mountain
To see what he could see.
But all that he could see,
But all that he could see
Was the other side of the mountain,
The other side of the mountain,
The other side of the mountain
Was all that he could see.

Beehive (Emilie Poulsson)

Here is the beehive.
(Hold up one fist.)
Where are the bees?
(Hand across eyebrows, looking.)
Hidden away where nobody sees.
(Point to closed hand.)
Here they come creeping out of the hive
One, two, three, four, five!
(Open up one finger for each number.)

Bingo (Traditional)

There was a farmer had a dog
And Bingo was his name-o.
B-I-N-G-O, B-I-N-G-O, B-I-N-G-O.
And Bingo was his name-o.
There was a farmer had a dog
And Bingo was his name-o.
(clap)-I-N-G-O, (clap)-I-N-G-O, (clap)-I-N-G-O.
And Bingo was his name-o.

(Repeat, clapping for an additional letter each
around until each letter in B-I-N-G-O is clapped.)

Bingo's Doghouse (Traditional)*

This is Bingo's doghouse,
(Touch fingers of each hand together to make
 a roof.)
This is Bingo's bed,
(Rub palm of hand with other hand, in
 smoothing motion.)
This is Bingo's pan of milk,
(Cup hands together.)
So that he can be fed.
(Imitate lapping milk like a dog.)
Bingo has a collar, with his name upon it, too.
(Circle neck with fingers.)
Take a stick and throw it,
(Imitate throwing.)
And he'll bring it back to you!
(Clap hands.)

Blastoff (Cynthia Holley)

Jump into your spacesuit,
Don't forget your hat.
(Imitate putting on suit and helmet.)
Climb into the rocketship
On the launching mat.
(Imitate climbing into ship and sitting down.)
Buckle up for takeoff.
Belts from head to toe.
(Imitate buckling safety belts.)
Countdown from ten and blastoff,
Up to the moon we go!
10, 9, 8, 7, 6, 5, 4, 3, 2, 1 . . . Blastoff!

Blow a Balloon (Cynthia Holley)

Here's a balloon without any air,
Flimsy as can be.
(Shake hand as if holding an unfilled balloon.)
What happens when we blow it up?
Let's try it out and see.
(Hold hands, palms up, looking puzzled.)
With a huff and a puff
And a great big blow,
(Imitate blowing balloon.)
It gets bigger and bigger.
Just watch it grow!
(Cup hands to make a balloon that grows
    bigger and bigger.)

Bow Belinda (Folk Song)

Bow, bow, bow Belinda,
Bow, bow, bow Belinda,
Bow, bow, bow Belinda,
Won't you be my darling?

Right hand up, oh Belinda,
Right hand up, oh Belinda,
Right hand up, oh Belinda,
Won't you be my darling?

Left hand up . . .

Both hands up . . .

Shake that big foot . . .

Promenade all . . .

(Form two lines, boys and girls facing each
other. On "bow Belinda," the boys bow and the
girls curtsy to partners. On "right hand up," they
take partner's hand, turn around each other, and
return to line. On "shake that big foot," they fold
hands across chest and pass around partners
back-to-back. On "promenade all," the head
couple makes arch with arms, and other couples
each join hands, pass under arch, then separate
and return to original line.)

Bow-wow Says the Dog
(Nursery Rhyme)

Whose dog art thou?
Little Tom Tinker's dog,
Bow-wow-wow!

Brother, Come and Dance with Me
(Humperdinck)

Brother, come and dance with me,
Both my hands I offer thee.
(Girls and boys face partners, extending and
    joining hands.)
Right foot first, left foot then,
(Step with right foot then left.)
Round about and back again.
(Turn in circle, holding hands of partner.)
With your foot you tap, tap, tap.
(Tap foot three times.)
With your hands you clap, clap, clap.
(Clap hands three times.)
Right foot first, left foot then,
(Step with right foot, then left.)
Round about and back again.
(Turn in circle, holding hands of partner.)

Bunny (Traditional)

Here is a bunny with ears so funny.
(Hold up first two fingers, slightly bent.)
And here is a hole in the ground.
(Place hand on hip forming opening with arm.)
When a noise he hears, he pricks up his ears,
(Quickly straighten first two fingers.)
And he jumps in the hole with a bound!
(Jump hand like a bunny through opening.)

The Bus Song (Traditional)

The wheels on the bus go round and round,
  round and round,
Round and round.
The wheels of the bus go round and round
All through the town.
(Roll hands round and round over each other.)

The horn on the bus goes beep-beep-beep,
  beep-beep-beep,
Beep-beep-beep.
The horn on the bus goes beep-beep-beep,
All through the town.
(Beep a horn.)

The wipers on the bus go swish-swish-swish,
  swish-swish-swish,
Swish-swish-swish.
The wipers on the bus go swish-swish-swish,
All through the town.
(Swish with forearms back and forth.)

The people on the bus go up and down, up and
  down,
Up and down,
The people on the bus go up and down,
All through the town.
(Stand up and sit back down.)

The money in the box goes ding-ding-ding,
 ding-ding-ding,
Ding-ding-ding,
The money in the box goes ding-ding-ding,
All through the town.
(Drop money into the box.)

The baby on the bus goes wah-wah-wah, wah-
 wah-wah,
Wah-wah-wah,
The baby on the bus goes wah-wah-wah,
All through the town.
(Rock baby in arms and say "wah!")

(Add other verses.)

Buttercups and Daisies

(Nursery Rhyme)

Buttercups and daisies,
Oh, the pretty flowers;
Coming ere the springtime,
To tell of sunny hours.
While the trees are leafless,
While the fields are bare,
Buttercups and daisies
Spring up here and there.

Bye Baby Bunting *(Nursery Rhyme)*

Bye baby bunting,
Daddy's gone a-hunting
To catch a little rabbit skin
To wrap my baby bunting in.

Can You Show Me How the Farmer?
(Adapted)

(TUNE: "DID YOU EVER SEE A LASSIE")

Can you show me how the farmer, the farmer,
 the farmer,
Can you show me how the farmer, how he
 plants his hay?
He plants this way and that way and this way
 and that way.
This is how the farmer, how he plants his hay.

Can you show me how the farmer . . . sows . . .

Can you show me how the farmer . . . reaps . . .

Can you show me how the farmer . . . bundles . . .

Can you show me how the farmer . . . carries . . .
(Imitate designated motion for each verse.)

Carpenter *(Adapted)*

Listen to the hammer go bang, bang, bang.
(Imitate hammering.)
Listen to the saw go zzzzzzzzzzz.
(Imitate sawing back and forth.)
Watch how the carpenter measures and
 screws,
(Imitate measuring and using screwdriver.)
As he builds a house for me!
(Touch fingers together to form roof.)

Caterpillar *(Traditional)*

Caterpillar, caterpillar, brown and furry,
(Move cupped hand along arm.)
Winter is coming and you'd better hurry.
(Move hand faster.)
Find a leaf under which to creep.
(Hold one hand over cupped hand.)
Spin a cocoon in which to sleep.
(Spin hand round and round cupped hand.)
Then when springtime comes one day,
(Open arms in large circular motion.)
You'll be a butterfly and fly away!
*(Hook thumbs and wave hands in flying
 motion.)*

Chickamy, Craney, Crow *(Traditional)*

Chickamy, chickamy, craney, crow,
I went to the well to wash my toe.
When I got back, my chickens were gone.
What time is it, old man?
It's ___o'clock!

 *(Children take turns tapping a bell or cymbal
as others count the number of times and chant,
replying with the time.)*

The Chimney *(Traditional)*

Here is the chimney.
(Hold up fist.)
Here is the top.
(Place flat hand on top of fist.)
Open the lid,
(Remove top hand.)
And out Santa will pop!
(Pop up thumb from fist.)

Choo-choo Train (Adapted)

Choo-choo-choo-choo,
The train puffs down the track.
(Bend arms at elbows and imitate chugging.)
Now it's going forward.
(Chug leaning forward.)
Now it's chugging back.
(Chug arms back to sitting position.)
Now the bell is ringing.
(Imitate ringing clapper of bell.)
Now the whistle blows.
(Imitate pulling chain of train whistle up and
  down.)
Chugging, chugging, chugging, chugging,
(Move bent arms back and forth.)
Down the track it goes!

Christmas Is Coming (Traditional)

Christmas is coming, the goose is getting fat,
Won't you please put a penny in the old man's
  hat?
If you haven't got a penny, a ha' penny will do,
If you haven't got a ha' penny, God bless you!

Christmastime (Adapted)

(TUNE: "ROW, ROW, ROW YOUR BOAT")

Ring, ring, ring the bells.
Ring them loud and clear.
(Imitate ringing bell with hand.)
Lights are shining everywhere.
Christmastime is near!
(Open and close hands like flashing lights.)

Clapping, Clapping, Softly Clapping (Traditional)

Clapping, clapping, softly clapping,
(Clap hands softly together.)
Turn them round and round.
(Turn hands one over the other.)
Clapping, clapping, softly clapping,
(Clap hands softly.)
Now put them quietly down!
(Lay hands quietly in lap.)

Clap with Me (Traditional)

Clap with me, 1, 2, 3.
Clap, clap, clap, just like me.
(Clap hands.)
Shake with me, 1, 2, 3.
Shake, shake, shake, just like me.
(Shake body.)
Roll with me, 1, 2, 3.
Roll, roll, roll, just like me.
(Roll hands one over the other.)

Snap with me, 1, 2, 3.
Snap, snap, snap, just like me.
(Snap fingers.)
Fold with me, 1, 2, 3.
Fold your hands, just like me.
(Fold hands and lay in lap.)

Clementine (Folk Song)

In a cavern, in a canyon, excavating for a mine,
Dwelt a miner, forty-niner, and his daughter,
  Clementine.
Oh, my darling, oh, my darling, oh, my darling
  Clementine,
You are lost and gone forever, dreadful sorrow,
  Clementine.

Clocks (Traditional)

Big clocks make a sound like t-i-c-k, t-o-c-k,
  t-i-c-k, t-o-c-k.
(Rest elbows on hips, extend arms, pointing
  index fingers, swaying arms back and
  forth rhythmically.)
Small clocks make a sound like tick, tock, tick,
  tock.
(Speak a little faster and move arms faster.)
And very tiny clocks make a sound like tick-
  tock-tick-tock!
(Move even faster.)
Tick-tock-tick-tock, tick, tock, tick t-o-c-k, t-i-c-k!
(Gradually slow down.)

Cobbler, Cobbler (Traditional)

Cobbler, cobbler, mend my shoe.
(Hold one foot across other knee.)
Have it done by half-past two.
(Hammer shoe with fist.)
Stitch it up and stitch it down.
(Imitate sewing motion.)
Now nail the heel all around.
(Hammer heel of shoe with fist.)

Cock-a-doodle-doo! (Nursery Rhyme)

Cock-a-doodle-doo,
My dame has lost her shoe.
My master's lost his fiddling stick.
And doesn't know what to do.
Cock-a-doodle-doo,
What's a dame to do?
Till master finds his fiddling stick,
She'll dance without her shoe.

Counting Balls (Traditional)*

Here's a ball.
(Put thumb and index finger together to form small circle.)
Here's a ball.
(Put hands together, touching thumbs and fingers.)
And here's a great big ball I see.
(Make circle with arms.)
Are you ready?
Shall we count them?
One, two, three!
(Remake each size ball.)

Creeping Indians (Traditional)

The Indians are creeping, shhhhhh.
(Tap two fingers on top of other hand; put finger to lips.)
The Indians are creeping, shhhhhh.
(Tap two fingers on top of other hand; put finger to lips.)
They do not make a sound as their feet touch the ground.
(Tap two fingers on top of other hand.)
The Indians are creeping, shhhhhh!
(Touch index finger to lips.)

Dancing Leaves (Adapted)

The autumn leaves come dancing down,
Yellow, red, gold, and brown.
(Wiggle fingers and move hands as if floating down.)
They make a carpet on the ground,
(Move hands as though smoothing ground.)
And fall asleep without a sound.
(Place hands together at face to imitate sleeping.)

Days of the Week (Adapted)

(TUNE: "YANKEE DOODLE")

Monday, Tuesday, Wednesday, Thursday,
Friday, Saturday, Sunday.
Let's all sing the days of the week
And learn them all by Monday!

Dentist (Traditional)

If I were a dentist,
I know what I would do.
(Point to self.)
I'd tell all the children, "Brush your teeth."
(Imitate brushing teeth.)
"Keep a smile like new."
(Make a big smile and point to lips.)
And if a tiny hole should show,
I'd say, "Climb into my chair."
(Make circle with fingers.)

I'd make my little drill go buzzzzzzzz,
And put a filling there!
(Point to teeth.)

Diddle, Diddle, Dumpling

(Nursery Rhyme)

Diddle, diddle, dumpling, my son John
Went to bed with his trousers on.
One shoe off and one shoe on,
Diddle, diddle, dumpling, my son John.

Did You Ever See a Lassie? (Traditional)

Did you ever see a lassie, a lassie, a lassie?
Did you ever see a lassie go this way and that?
Go this way and that way, and this way and that way.
Did you ever see a lassie go this way and that?

(Children form a circle with one child in center. "It" demonstrates a movement such as clapping, stamping, or swaying, and others imitate.)

Dig a Little Hole (Traditional)

Dig a little hole.
(Imitate digging motion.)
Plant a little seed.
(Imitate dropping seed.)
Pour a little water.
(Imitate pouring.)
And pull a little weed.
(Imitate pulling motion.)

Ding, Dong Bell (Nursery Rhyme)

Ding, dong bell, Pussy's in the well!
Who put her in? Little Tommy Green.
Who pulled her out? Little Tommy Stout.
What a naughty boy was that,
To try to drown poor pussy cat,
Who never did him any harm,
But frightened mice in his father's barn!

Dinosaurs (Cynthia Holley)*

(TUNE: "LONDON BRIDGE")

Dinosaurs lived long ago, long ago, long ago,
Dinosaurs lived long ago,
That's prehistoric!

Tyrannosaurus was very mean, very mean, very mean,
Tyrannosaurus was very mean,
That's prehistoric!

Brontosaurus was very big, very big, very big,
Brontosaurus was very big,
That's prehistoric!

Stegosaurus wore heavy spikes, heavy spikes,
  heavy spikes,
Stegosaurus wore heavy spikes,
That's prehistoric!

Triceratops had big sharp horns, big sharp
  horns, big sharp horns,
Triceratops had big sharp horns,
That's prehistoric!

Pteranodon could fly in the air, fly in the air, fly
  in the air,
Pteranodon could fly in the air,
That's prehistoric!

All the dinosaurs disappeared, disappeared,
  disappeared,
All the dinosaurs disappeared,
That's prehistoric!

Don't Let the Dragons Get You
(Cynthia Holley)

The dragons are coming to town tonight.
Watch out, be careful; they're looking to fight.
Big balls of fire from their mouths they will blow,
And scales of green on their body will glow.
They like to sneak and they hide in the trees,
Walking along on their hands and their knees.
Oh, no, he's got me! Help! What can I do?
Oh, no, watch out! Now he's coming for you!

Don't Worry If Your Job Is Small
(Anonymous)

Don't worry if your job is small,
And your rewards are few.
Remember that the mighty oak,
Was once a nut like you.

Donut Song *(Traditional)*

(Tune: "Turkey in the Straw")

Oh, I walked 'round the corner and I walked
  'round the block,
And I walked right into a donut shop,
And I picked up a donut and I wiped off the
  grease,
And I handed the lady a five-cent piece.
Well, she looked at the nickel and she looked at
  me,
And she said, "Hey kid, can't you plainly see?
There's a hole in the nickel, there's a hole right
  through!"
And I said, "There's a hole in the donut too!
Thanks for the donut! Good day!"

Down by the Station *(Traditional)*

Down by the station early in the morning,
See the little train cars all in a row.
Listen to the engineer pull the big whistle.
Toot-toot, toot-toot! Off we go!

Do Your Ears Hang Low? *(Traditional)*

Do your ears hang low?
Do they wobble to and fro?
Can you tie them in a knot?
Can you tie them in a bow?
Can you fling them over your shoulder
Like a continental soldier?
Do your ears hang low?

Dragon Hunt *(Adapted)*

We're going on a dragon hunt, don't be afraid.
(Slap thighs in rhythm.)
Oh no, I see a swamp!
(Hand across eyebrows.)
Can't go under it, can't go over it, have to go
  through it.
OK, put on our boots,
(Imitate putting on boots.)
Slush, slush, slush, slush, slush!
(Imitate tromping through mud.)

We're going on a dragon hunt, don't be afraid.
(Slap thighs in rhythm.)
Oh no, I see a stream!
(Hand across eyebrows.)
Can't go under it, can't go over it, have to go
  through it.
OK, put on our swimsuits,
(Imitate putting on swimsuits.)
Splash, splash, splash, splash, splash!
(Imitate swimming.)

We're going on a dragon hunt, don't be afraid.
(Slap thighs in rhythm.)
Oh no, I see a tree!
(Hand across eyebrows.)
Can't go under it, can't go over it, let's climb it.
(Imitate climbing tree and sliding down.)

We're going on a dragon hunt, don't be afraid.
(Slap thighs in rhythm.)
Oh no, I see a cave!
(Hand across eyebrows.)
Can't go under it, can't go over it, let's go inside.
(Imitate creeping into a cave.)

It's dark.
(Move hands as though feeling in dark.)
I think I hear something.
(Put hand to ear.)
I think I see something.
(Hand across eyebrows.)
Look out! It's a dragon!

(Run back, repeating above verses in reverse.
When you arrive home, ask "Who was afraid?")

Eenie, Meenie, Minie, Moe (Traditional)

Eenie, meenie, minie, moe,
Catch a tiger by the toe.
If he hollers let him go,
Eenie, meenie, minie, moe.

Eensy, Weensy Spider (Traditional)

The eensy, weensy spider went up the water
spout.
(With thumb touching little finger of other hand,
climb fingers.)
Down came the rain and washed the spider out.
(Motion hands downward and out.)
Out came the sun and dried up all the rain.
(Form circle with arms overhead.)
And the eensy, weensy spider went up the
spout again.
(Repeat climbing with fingers.)

The Evening Is Coming (Anonymous)

The evening is coming.
The sun sinks to rest.
The birds are all flying
Straight home to their nests.
"Caw, caw," says the crow
As he flies overhead.
It's time little children
Were going to bed.

Here comes the pony.
His work is all done.
Down through the meadow
He takes a good run.
Up go his heels,
And down goes his head.
It's time little children
Were going to bed.

Eye Winker (Traditional)

Eye winker,
(Point to eyes.)
Tom Tinker,
(Point to ears.)
Nose smeller,
(Point to nose.)

Mouth eater,
(Point to mouth.)
Chin chopper,
(Point to chin.)
Chin chopper, chin chopper, chin chopper, chin!

Farmer (Traditional)

First the farmer sows his seeds.
(Imitate planting seeds.)
Then he stands and takes his ease.
(Stand with hands on hips.)
He stamps his foot.
(Stamp foot.)
He claps his hands,
(Clap hands.)
And turns around to view his lands.
(Turn around with hand across eyebrows,
looking.)

The Farmer in the Dell (Traditional)

The farmer in the dell,
The farmer in the dell,
Hi-ho and merry-o,
The farmer in the dell.
The farmer takes a wife.
The farmer takes a wife.
Hi-ho and merry-o,
The farmer takes a wife.

The wife takes the child . . .

The child takes the nurse . . .

The nurse takes the dog . . .

The dog takes the cat . . .

The cat takes the rat . . .

The rat takes the cheese . . .

The cheese stands alone.
The cheese stands alone.
Hi-ho and merry-o,
The cheese stands alone.

(Children walk in a circle holding hands. The
farmer selects one child to be his wife, the wife
selects the child, etc. When the class sings "the
cheese stands alone," everyone but the cheese
returns to the circle.)

Fee, Fie, Foe, Fum *(Cynthia Holley)*

Fee, fie, foe, fum,
Here comes a dragon,
Let's all run.
Fee, fie, foe, fum,
He's not blowing smoke,
It's bubble gum,
Fee, fie, foe, fum,
He only wants to have some fun!

Fine Family *(Traditional)*

Here is the family in my household.
(Hold up five fingers.)
Some are young,
(Move thumb.)
And some are old.
(Move index finger.)
Some are tall,
(Move middle finger.)
Some are small.
(Move ring finger.)
Some are growing just like me.
(Move little finger.)
Together we all live as a family.
(Move all five fingers.)

Finger Band *(Traditional)*

The finger band has come to town,
The finger band has come to town,
The finger band has come to town,
So early in the morning.

The finger band can play the drums . . .

The finger band can play the flute . . .

The finger band can play the horn . . .

The finger band can play the bells . . .

The finger band has gone away . . .

(Imitate playing the various instruments.)

Fingers, Fingers, Everywhere *(Adapted)*

Fingers, fingers everywhere,
Fingers blinking in the air,
(Wiggle fingers, open and shut hands.)
Fingers reach to touch ten toes,
Fingers tying little bows,
(Touch toes and imitate tying.)
Fingers learn to button and snap,
(Imitate buttoning and snapping.)
Fingers, fingers, clap, clap, clap!
(Clap hands three times.)

Firefighter *(Cynthia Holley)*

(TUNE: "EENSY, WEENSY SPIDER")

The firefighter helps us learn our safety rules.
Playing with matches is only for fools.
If you see a fire, "Help," you'll scream and
shout.
Dial 911. The firefighter will put it out.

Fireflies *(Traditional)*

Winking, blinking, winking, blinking,
(Open and shut hand.)
See that little light.
(Open and shut hand.)
Now it's here and now it's there,
*(Open and close hand near body, then away
from body.)*
Now it's out of sight.
(Hide hand behind back.)
Winking, blinking, winking, blinking,
(Open and shut hand.)
Fireflies at night.

Five Big Elephants *(Traditional)*

Five big elephants, oh, what a sight!
(Hold up five fingers.)
Swinging their trunks from left to right.
(Clasp hands and swing arms back and forth.)
Four are followers, and one is the king.
(Hold up four fingers, then thumb.)
They all walk around in the circus ring!
*(Clasp hands and swing arms and lumber like
an elephant.)*

Five Big Indians *(Traditional)*

There were five great big Indians.
They stood so straight and tall.
They tried to fit in a little canoe,
And one of them did fall.

There were four great big Indians . . .

There were three great big Indians . . .

There were two great big Indians . . .

There was one great big Indian.
He stood so straight and tall,
And *he* did fit in the little canoe,
And he paddled it right home.

*(Hold up appropriate number of fingers for each
verse. Imitate paddling for last verse.)*

Five Birthday Candles *(Cynthia Holley)*

Five birthday candles on my special cake,
Sorry I can't tell you the wish I'll make.
Everybody ready to sing "Happy Birthday"?
We'll blow all the candles out and shout
    "Hooray"!
Whew! whew, whew, whew, whew, Hooray!

(Hold up five fingers and blow each down. Hold up fist for "Hooray!")

Five Funny Speckled Frogs

(Traditional)*

Five funny speckled frogs sat on a spotted log,
Eating the most delicious bugs, YUM, YUM!
One jumped into a pool, where it was nice and
    cool.
Then there were four funny speckled frogs.

Four funny speckled frogs . . .

Three funny speckled frogs . . .

Two funny speckled frogs . . .

One funny speckled frog sat on a spotted log,
Eating the most delicious bugs, YUM, YUM!
He jumped into the pool, where it was nice and
    cool,
Then there were no more speckled frogs!

(Hold out arm for log and place five fingers of other hand on top. Jump with hand into pool and return hand with appropriate number of fingers for each verse. Rub tummy for "YUM, YUM!")

Five Huge Dinosaurs *(Cynthia Holley)**

Five huge dinosaurs lived long ago.
The Tyrannosaurus went to war,
And then there were four.

Four huge dinosaurs lived long ago.
The Brontosaurus munched a tree,
And then there were three.

Three huge dinosaurs lived long ago.
The Pterandon up away he flew,
And then there were two.

Two huge dinosaurs lived long ago.
The Struthiomimus far away did run,
And then there was one.

One huge dinosaur lived long ago.
The Plesiosaur left to swim and sun,
And then there were none.

(Hold up appropriate number of fingers for each verse.)

Five Kittens *(Traditional)*

Five little kittens standing in a row,
(Hold up five fingers.)
They nod their heads to the children so.
(Bend fingers forward.)
They run to the left; they run to the right.
(Wiggle and move fingers to left, then right.)
They stand up and stretch in the bright sunlight.
(Slowly stretch up fingers.)
Along comes a dog who's in for some fun.
(Move fist of other hand towards fingers.)
ME-OW! See those little kittens run!
(Fingers run away and hide behind back.)

Five Little Babies *(Cynthia Holley)**

Five little babies were playing together one day.
One saw a big ball, and so he crawled away.

Four little babies were playing together one day.
One saw a rattle, and she crawled away.

Three little babies were playing together one
    day.
One saw a kitty cat, and he crawled away.

Two little babies were playing together one day.
One saw a teddy bear, and she crawled away.

One little baby was playing by himself one day.
He cried and his mommy came and took him
    away.

(Hold up and fold down appropriate number of fingers for each verse.)

Five Little Bears *(Traditional)**

Five little cubby bears, tumbling on the ground,
(Roll hands over each other.)
The first little bear said, "Let's look around."
(Hold up thumb.)
The second one said, "See the little bunny."
(Hold up index finger.)
The third one said, "I smell honey!"
(Hold up middle finger.)
The fourth one said, "It's over in the trees."
(Hold up ring finger.)
The fifth one said, "Look out! Here come the
    bees!"
(Hold up little finger, while fingers of other hand imitate buzzing.)

Five Little Bells *(Traditional)**

Five little bells hanging in a row.
(Hold up five fingers.)
The first one said, "Ring me slow."
(Move thumb slowly.)
The second one said, "Ring me fast."
(Wiggle index finger.)
The third one said, "Ring me last."
(Move middle finger.)
The fourth one said, "I'm like a chime."
(Move ring finger.)
And the fifth one said, "Ring us all. It's
  Christmastime!"
(Wiggle all five fingers.)

Five Little Chickens *(Traditional)**

Said the first little chicken with a queer little
  squirm,
"Oh, I wish I could find a fat little worm!"

Said the second little chicken with an odd little
  shrug,
"Oh, I wish I could find a fat little bug!"

Said the third little chicken with a little sigh of
  grief,
"Oh, I wish I could find a green little leaf!"

Said the fourth little chicken with a sharp little
  squeal,
"Oh, I wish I could find some nice yellow meal!"

Said the fifth little chicken with a faint little
  moan,
"Oh, I wish I could find a wee gravel stone!"

"Now see here!" said their mother from the
  green garden patch,
"If you want any breakfast, you just come here
  and scratch!"

*(Hold up appropriate number of fingers for each
verse. Scratch with fingers for last verse.)*

Five Little Clowns *(Cynthia Holley)**

Five little clowns on the circus floor—
One did a somersault; then there were four.

Four little clowns standing on one knee—
One fell over backwards; then there were three.

Three little clowns with hair of red and blue—
One rode on an elephant; then there were two.

Two little clowns having so much fun—
One flew on the trapeze; then there was one.

One little clown in the ring all alone—
He stood on a tiger and ate an ice cream cone!

*(Hold up appropriate number of fingers for each
verse.)*

Five Little Ducks *(Traditional)**

Five little ducks went swimming one day
Over the pond and far away.
Mama Duck said, "Quack, quack, quack,"
And only four little ducks came back.

Four little ducks . . .

Three little ducks . . .

Two little ducks . . .

One little duck . . . And no little duck came
  swimming back.

Mama Duck went swimming one day,
Over the pond and far away.
Mama Duck said, "Quack, quack, quack,"
And five little ducks came swimming back!

*(Hold up the appropriate number of fingers for
each verse. Put palms together to "quack.")*

Five Little Easter Rabbits *(Traditional)*

Five little Easter rabbits sitting by the door—
One hopped away, and then there were four.
Refrain:
Hop, hop, hop, hop, see how they run!
Hop, hop, hop, hop. They think it's great fun!

Four little Easter rabbits under a tree—
One hopped away, and then there were three.
(Repeat refrain.)

Three little Easter rabbits, looking at you—
One hopped away, and then there were two.
(Repeat refrain.)

Two little Easter rabbits resting in the sun—
One hopped away, and then there was one.
(Repeat refrain.)

One little Easter rabbit left all alone—
He hopped away and then there were none!
(Repeat refrain.)

*(Hold up appropriate number of fingers for each
verse. For refrain, hold up two fingers and hop
with hand like a bunny.)*

Five Little Farmers (Traditional)

Five little farmers woke up with the sun,
(Stretch arms up, as if awakening.)
For it was early morning and chores must be done.
(Yawn.)
The first little farmer went to milk the cow.
(Imitate milking cow.)
The second little farmer thought he'd better plow.
(Imitate plowing.)
The third little farmer fed the hungry hens.
(Imitate throwing feed.)
The fourth little farmer mended broken pens.
(Imitate hammering.)
The fifth little farmer took his vegetables to town,
(Imitate driving.)
Baskets filled with cabbages, and sweet potatoes brown.
(Imitate carrying heavy baskets.)
When the work was finished and the western sky was red,
(Point to sky.)
Five little farmers tumbled into bed!
(Hands at cheek imitating sleeping.)

Five Little Leaves (Adapted)*

Five little leaves, so bright and gay,
Hung on a tree one nice fall day.
The wind came blowing 'round and 'round,
And one little leaf came tumbling down.

Four little leaves . . .

Three little leaves . . .

Two little leaves . . .

One little leaf . . .

(Raise forearm as tree, and put up appropriate number of fingers for each verse. Use other hand to whirl around tree like the wind.)

Five Little Magnets (Cynthia Holley)*

Five little magnets, shiny and new,
Let us see, what can they do?
The first little magnet picked up a nail.
The second little magnet took the lid from a pail.
The third little magnet attracted a tack.
The fourth got a buckle painted black.
The fifth little magnet was really strong;
It caught a rod of metal five feet long!

(Hold up five fingers, point to each finger as appropriate.)

Five Little Mice (Traditional)

Five little mice on the pantry floor:
(Hold up five fingers.)
This little mouse peeked behind the door;
(Bend down little finger.)
This little mouse nibbled at the cake;
(Bend down ring finger.)
This little mouse not a sound did make;
(Bend down middle finger.)
This little mouse took a bite of cheese;
(Bend down index finger.)
This little mouse heard a kitten sneeze.
(Bend down thumb.)
"Ah-choo!" sneezed the kitten, and "Squeak," they cried,
(Imitate sneezing and startling.)
as they found a hole and ran inside.
(Put hand on opposite hip, making a hole, and run fingers through the hole.)

Five Little Monkeys Jumping on the Bed
(Traditional)

Five little monkeys jumping on the bed.
One fell off and bumped his head.
His mother called the doctor, and the doctor said,
"No more monkeys jumping on the bed!"

Four little monkeys . . .

Three little monkeys . . .

Two little monkeys . . .

One little monkey jumping on the bed.
He fell off and bumped his head.
Then there were no more monkeys to jump on the bed!

Five Little Monkeys Swinging in a Tree
(Traditional)

Five little monkeys swinging in a tree,
Teasing Mr. Alligator—"Can't catch me."
Along comes Mr. Alligator, happy as can be
And SNAP! Four monkeys!

Four little monkeys . . .

Three little monkeys . . .

Two little monkeys . . .

One little monkey . . . SNAP! No more monkeys!

(Hold up and swing five fingers; make alligator mouth with other hand to "snap" up the monkeys.)

Five Little Pilgrims (Traditional)*

Five little Pilgrims on Thanksgiving Day:
The first one said, "I'll have corn if I may."
The second one said, "I'll have turkey roasted."
The third one said, "I'll have chestnuts toasted."
The fourth one said, "I'll have pumpkin pie."
The fifth one said, "Oh, cranberries I spy."
But before the Pilgrims ate their turkey
  dressing,
They bowed their heads and said a Thanks-
  giving blessing.

(Hold up appropriate number of fingers for each line; bow heads for last line.)

Five Little Presents (Adapted)

The first little present goes to Patrick.
The second little present goes to Shaun.
The third little present goes to Eric.
The fourth little present goes to Dawn.
And the last little present cried, "Boo, hoo, hoo,
I want to go into a stocking too!"

(Hold up five fingers, moving one at a time for each line.)

Five Little Pumpkins (Traditional)*

Five little pumpkins sitting on a gate,
(Hold up five fingers.)
The first one said, "Oh my, it's getting late."
(Hold up thumb.)
The second one said, "There are witches in the
  air."
(Hold up index finger.)
The third one said, "I don't care."
(Hold up middle finger.)
The fourth one said, "Let's run, run, run."
(Hold up ring finger.)
The fifth one said, "It's Halloween fun."
(Hold up little finger.)
Then woooooooooooo went the wind,
(Wave hands back and forth.)
And OUT went the light!
(Clap hands loudly.)
Five little pumpkins rolled out of sight.
(Roll hands one over the other.)

Five Little Puppies (Traditional)*

This little puppy said, "Let's go out to play."
This little puppy said, "Let's run away."
This little puppy said, "Let's stay out till dark."
This little puppy said, "Let's bark, bark, bark."
This little puppy said, "I think it would be fun
To go straight home. Let's run, run, run!"

(Hold up five fingers, point to a finger for each puppy, and run fingers behind back for last line.)

Five Little Seashells (Adapted)*

Five little seashells sleeping on the shore—
Swish! went a big wave, and then there
  were four.

Four little seashells quiet as can be—
Swish! went a big wave, and then there
  were three.

Three little seashells pearly and new—
Swish! went a big wave, and then there
  were four

Two little seashells lying in the sun—
Swish! went a big wave, and then there was
  one.

One little seashell left all alone—
Swish! went a big wave, and then there
  were none.

Five little seashells gone out to sea,
Wait until morning and they'll return to me.

(Hold up five fingers, bending down one finger for each verse. Move arms, palms out to make the waves. Point out to sea, then to self for last verse.)

Five Little Snowmen (Traditional)*

Five little snowmen standing in a row—
(Hold up five fingers.)
Each with a hat and a big red bow.
(Point to head and neck.)
Five little snowmen dressed for show—
(Smooth clothes with hands.)
Now they are ready. Where will they go?
(Put hand across eyebrows, looking.)
Wait 'til the sun shines. Then they will go
(Hold arms in circle overhead.)
Down through the fields with the melting
  snow.
(Pretend to melt away.)

Five Little Squirrels (Traditional)

Five little squirrels sitting in a tree:
The first squirrel said, "What do I see?"
The second squirrel said, "I see a gun!"
The third squirrel said, "Oh, let's run!"
The fourth squirrel said, "Let's hide in the
  shade."
The fifth one said, "I'm not afraid."
Then BANG went the gun, and away they
  did run.

(Hold up five fingers, moving one finger for each line. Clap hands together at "BANG," and run fingers behind back.)

Five Little Valentines *(Cynthia Holley)* *

Five little valentines left at the door—
The red one was for mother; then there were
four.

Four little valentines sitting quietly—
The green one was for brother; then there were
three.

Three little valentines, yellow, pink, and blue—
Sister took the pink one; that left two.

Two little valentines, oh what fun—
The blue one was for Daddy; then there was
one.

One little valentine—who should know
My favorite color? It is yellow!

Five little hearts on Valentine's Day—
Each says "I love you!" in a special way.

*(Hold up five fingers, moving one finger for
each verse.)*

Five Pretty Easter Eggs *(Adapted)* *

Five pretty Easter eggs in a basket by the
door—
Mother ate the red one; then there were four.

Four pretty Easter eggs hidden behind a tree—
Brother ate the green one; then there were
three.

Three pretty Easter eggs, yellow, pink, and
blue—
Sister ate the yellow one; then there were two.

Two pretty Easter eggs lying in the sun—
Daddy ate the blue one; then there was but
one.

One pretty Easter egg sitting by itself—
I took that pretty Easter egg and put it on the
shelf!

*(Hold up five fingers, moving one finger for
each verse.)*

The Flower *(Traditional)*

Here's a green leaf,
(Show one cupped hand.)
And here's a green leaf.
(Show other cupped hand.)
That you see makes two.
Here is a bud that makes a flower,
(Cup hands together.)
Watch it bloom for you!
*(Gradually open hands, spread fingers like
flower.)*

For He's (She's) a Jolly Good Fellow *(Traditional)*

For he's (she's) a jolly good fellow,
For he's (she's) a jolly good fellow,
For he's (she's) a jolly good fellow,
Which nobody can deny.
Which nobody can deny,
Which nobody can deny.

(Repeat.)

Four Little Monkeys *(Traditional)*

Two little monkeys, sitting in a tree
Were joined by another, and that made three.

Three little monkeys in the tree did play.
They chattered and chattered in a happy way.

Three little monkeys wishing for one more;
Another came to join them, and that made four.

Monkeys, monkeys, how many do I see?
Four little monkeys, sitting in a tree.

*(Hold up appropriate number of fingers for
each verse.)*

Four Seasons *(Anonymous)*

Spring is showery, flowery, bowery.
Summer: hoppy, choppy, poppy.
Autumn: wheezy, sneezy, freezy.
Winter: slippy, drippy, nippy.

Foxes in Their Den *(Adapted)*

1, 2, 3, 4, 5 in a row,
The foxes in their den.
(Hold up fingers one at a time.)
Sitting right beside them
Are 7, 8, 9, and 10!
(Hold up other five fingers.)

Frère Jacques (Traditional French)

Frère Jacques, Frère Jacques,
Dormez vous? Dormez vous?
Sonnez les matines, sonnez les matines,
Din, dan, don, din, dan, don.

Are You Sleeping?
(Translation from French)

Are you sleeping, are you sleeping,
Brother John? Brother John?
Morning bells are ringing, morning bells are
   ringing.
Ding, ding, dong, ding, ding, dong.

Fuzzy Wuzzy (Traditional)

Fuzzy Wuzzy was a bear.
Fuzzy Wuzzy had no hair.
Then Fuzzy Wuzzy wasn't fuzzy, was he?

Georgy Porgy (Nursery Rhyme)

Georgy Porgy, pudding and pie,
Kissed the girls and made them cry.
When the boys came out to play,
Georgy Porgy ran away.

The Ghost (Cynthia Holley)

I'm a big white ghost with black, scary eyes.
(Make two circles with fingers as eyes.)
Watch out now for a big surprise.
(Hand across eyebrows, looking.)
I'll fly through the sky until I find you,
(Imitate flying.)
And quietly sneak up and whisper, "BOO!"
(Imitate sneaking up.)

Go In and Out the Window (Folk Song)

Go in and out the window, go in and out the
   window,
Go in and out the window as we have done
   before.
(Repeat.)

*(Children sing as they walk slowly with hands
joined and held up high. One child goes in and
out under the arms of the others, skipping
through the circle.)*

Golden Fishes (Adapted)

Golden fishes swimming, floating,
Swimming, floating all the day,
Golden fishes in a school they travel,
Down in the ocean and down by the bay.

*(Hold palms of hands together, imitating
swimming fish.)*

Good Morning to You (Traditional)

Good morning to you, good morning to you,
Good morning everybody, good morning to you.

Good Night (Traditional)

Two little hands go clap, clap, clap.
Two little arms lie in my lap.
Two little feet go bump, bump, bump.
Two little legs give one big jump.
Two little eyes are shut up tight.
One little voice whispers soft, "Good night."
*(Move as words direct. Put hands together at
cheeks, imitating sleeping for last line.)*

Grandmother's Glasses (Traditional)

Here are grandmother's glasses.
(Put fingers around eyes.)
Here is grandmother's hat.
(Hands in triangle on head.)
And this is the way she folds her hands
(Fold hands together.)
And puts them in her lap.
(Place folded hands in lap.)
Here are grandpa's glasses.
(Put fingers around eyes.)
Here is grandpa's hat.
(Hands in triangle on head.)
And here is the way he folds his arms,
(Cross arms in front of chest.)
Just like that!

Grasshoppers (Adapted)

Grasshopper Green is a comical chap;
He lives on the best of fare.
Bright little trousers, jacket, and cap—
These are his springtime wear.
Out in the meadow he loves to go,
Playing in the sun.
Refrain:
It's hopperty, skipperty, high and low,
Spring is the time for fun.

Grasshopper Green has a dozen wee boys,
And as soon as their legs are strong,
Each of them joins in his frolicsome joys,
Singing his merry song.
Under the hedge they love to go,
As soon as the day has begun.
(Repeat refrain.)

Grasshopper Green has a quaint little house;
It's under the hedge so gay.
Grandmother Spider, as still as a mouse,
Watches him over the way.
Gladly he's calling the children, I know,
Out in the beautiful sun.
(Repeat refrain.)

Hammering *(Adapted)*

Bang, bang, bang with your hammer.
  (Make fist and bang with thumb pointed up.)
Pound, pound, pound, pound the nail.
(Pound nail with fist.)
Twist, twist, twist with your big wrench.
(Imitate turning wrench.)
Paint with your paintbrush and pail.
(Imitate painting.)

Hands on Shoulders *(Traditional)*

Hands on shoulders, hands on knees,
Hands behind you if you please.
Touch your shoulders, now your nose,
Now your chin and now your toes.
Hands up high in the air,
Down at your sides, and touch your hair.
Hands up high as before,
Now clap your hands—one, two, three, four.

(Follow action indicated.)

Hanukkah Candles *(Cynthia Holley)*

The menorah shines so pretty and bright,
*(Cup hands, joining at wrists to form a
  menorah.)*
With eight little candles for me to light.
(Hold up eight fingers.)
Eight little candles twinkle and shine;
(Wiggle fingers.)
Special presents soon will be mine.
(Point to self.)
Hanukkah candles glow, glow, glow—
(Wiggle fingers again.)
Remind us of days so long ago.

Have You Ever Seen? *(Anonymous)*

Have you ever seen a sheet on a river bed?
Or a single hair from a hammer's head?
Has the foot of a mountain any toes?
And is there a pair of garden hose?

Does the needle ever blink its eye?
Why doesn't the wing of a building fly?
Can you tickle the ribs of a parasol?
Or open the trunk of a tree at all?

Are the teeth of a rake ever going to bite?
Have the hands of a clock any left or right?
Can the garden plot be deep and dark?
And what is the sound of the birch's bark?

Head, Shoulders, Knees, and Toes
(Traditional)

My head, my shoulders, my knees, my toes.
My head, my shoulders, my knees, my toes.
My head, my shoulders, my knees, my toes.
My head, my shoulders, my knees, my toes.
Let's all clap hands together. *(clap, clap)*

*(Children touch parts as named. Other parts
can be interchanged—eyes, nose, fingers, toes—
as desired.)*

Here Are My Lady's Knives and Forks
(Traditional)

Here are my lady's knives and forks.
(Interlock fingers to indicate knives and forks.)
Here is father's table.
*(Keeping fingers interlocked, turn hands over
  so fingers form tabletop and wrists form legs.)*
Here is sister's looking glass.
(Raise one hand, fingers forming circle, to eye.)
And here is baby's cradle.
(Rocks hands like a cradle.)

Here Is Baby's Tossled Head
(Traditional)

Here is baby's tossled head,
(Make a fist.)
He nods, and nods,
(Bend wrist, bobbing fist up and down.)
Let's put him to bed.
(Bend other arm and tuck fist in at elbow.)

Here's a Ball *(Cynthia Holley)*

Here's a ball I throw it high.
Look, it almost touched the sky.
(Imitate throwing ball up.)
Now I bounce it on the ground,
Boom, boom, boom, boom, what a sound.
(Imitate bouncing ball.)
Now I roll it gently so.
(Imitate rolling ball.)
Watch, let's see where it will go.
(Hand across eyebrows, looking.)

Here's a Cup of Tea *(Traditional)*

Here's a cup, and here's a cup,
(Make a circle with thumb and index fingers.)
And here's a pot of tea.
*(Make fist with one hand, extending thumb for
  spout.)*

Pour a cup, and pour a cup,
(Imitate pouring with fist.)
And have a drink with me.
(Imitate sipping from cup.)

Here's a Hill *(Adapted)*

Here's a hill,
(Hold out bent arm.)
All covered with snow.
(Rub hand over arm.)
And here is the sled,
(Put fist of other hand on arm.)
SWISH, watch it go!
(Slide fist down arm.)

Here Sits a Monkey *(Traditional)*

Here sits a monkey in a chair, chair, chair.
He lost all the true loves he had last year.
So rise up on your feet and greet the first
  you meet,
The happiest one I know.

*(The "monkey" sits on a chair as others walk
around it in a circle. He or she stands up, shakes
hands, and selects a new monkey.)*

He's Got the Whole World *(Traditional)*

He's got the whole world in his hands.
He's got the whole wide world in his hands.
He's got the whole world in his hands.
He's got the whole world in his hands.

*(Repeat, substituting "little bitty baby," "you and
me brother," "you and me sister," "everybody.")*

Hey Diddle, Diddle *(Nursery Rhyme)*

Hey diddle, diddle, the cat and the fiddle,
The cow jumped over the moon.
The little dog laughed to see such a sport,
And the dish ran away with the spoon.

Hey Lolly, Lolly *(Adapted)*

I know a boy; his name is Billy.
Hey Lolly, Lolly Lo.
B-i-l-l-y spells Billy,
Hey, Lolly, Lolly lo.
Hey, Lolly, Lolly, Lolly,
Hey, Lolly, Lolly lo.
Hey, Lolly, Lolly, Lolly,
Hey, Lolly, Lolly lo!

(Repeat, spelling children's names.)

Hickory Dickory Dock *(Nursery Rhyme)*

Hickory dickory dock.
The mouse ran up the clock.
The clock struck one.
The mouse ran down.
Hickory dickory dock. TICK, TOCK!

Higgety-Piggety, My Black Hen
(Nursery Rhyme)

Higgety-piggety, my black hen, she lays eggs
  for gentlemen,
Sometimes nine and sometimes ten,
Higgety-piggety, my black hen.

Hippety Hop to the Barber Shop
(Nursery Rhyme)

Hippety hop to the barber shop,
To buy a stick of candy.
One for you and one for me,
And one for sister Annie.

Hokey Pokey *(Traditional)*

You put your right hand in, you put your right
  hand out,
You put your right hand in, and you shake it all
  about.
You do the Hokey Pokey and you turn yourself
  around,
That's what it's all about.
*(Imitate named movements, waving fingers and
  turning around for the "Hokey Pokey.")*

You put your left hand . . .

You put your right foot . . .

You put your left foot . . .

You put your head . . .

You put your whole self . . .

You do the Hokey Pokey, you do the Hokey
  Pokey,
You do the Hokey Pokey. That's what it's all
  about!

Home on the Range
(Traditional Cowboy)

Oh, give me a home where the buffalo roam,
And the deer and the antelope play,
Where seldom is heard a discouraging word,
And the skies are not cloudy all day.
Home, home on the range, where the deer and
  the antelope play,
Where seldom is heard a discouraging word,
And the skies are not cloudy all day.

Hot Cross Buns *(Nursery Rhyme)*

Hot cross buns, hot cross buns.
One penny, two penny, hot cross buns.

The House *(Traditional)*

This is the roof of the house so good.
*(Hold up hands, palms facing, and slant fingers
  to touch fingertips.)*
These are the walls that are made of wood.
(Extend hands parallel.)
These are the windows that let in the light.
*(Make a square by extending index fingers up,
  thumbs out.)*
This is the door that shuts so tight.
(Make bigger square.)
This is the chimney so straight and tall.
(Raise index finger.)
What a good house for us, one and all!
(Hold out fingers, parallel to each other.)

Houses *(Traditional)*

Here is the nest for robin.
(Cup hands together.)
Here is a hive for the bee.
(Make a fist.)
Here is a hole for the bunny.
(Finger and thumb touch to make a circle.)
And here is a house for me!
*(Hold up hands, palms facing, and slant fingers
  to put fingertips together.)*

Humpty Dumpty *(Nursery Rhyme)*

Humpty Dumpty sat on the wall;
Humpty Dumpty had a great fall.
All the king's horses and all the king's men
Couldn't put Humpty together again.

Hush, Little Baby *(Traditional Lullaby)* *

Hush, little baby, don't say a word,
Papa's going to buy you a mockingbird.
And if that mockingbird don't sing,
Papa's going to buy you a diamond ring.

If that diamond ring turns brass,
Papa's going to buy you a looking glass.
If that looking glass gets broke,
Papa's going to buy you a billy goat.
If that billy goat won't pull,
Papa's going to buy you a cart and bull.
If that cart and bull turns over,
Papa's going to buy you a dog named Rover.
If that dog named Rover won't bark,
Papa's going to buy you a horse and cart.
If that horse and cart fall down,
You'll still be the prettiest baby in town.

I Am a Fine Musician *(Traditional)*

I am a fine musician. I practice every day.
And people come from miles around just to
  hear me play . . .
My trumpet, my trumpet,
I love to play my trumpet.
Toot, toot, toot, toot, toot, toot,
Toot, toot, toot, toot, toot, toot.

. . . My trombone . . .

. . . My big drum . . .

. . . My cymbals . . .

*(Add other verses. Children imitate instrument
sounds as they sing.)*

I Am an Elephant *(Adapted)*

I am an elephant so big and strong,
*(Stand hunched over, arms down, hands
  clasped.)*
I swing my trunk as I walk along.
(Swing arms back and forth, hands clasped.)
I can walk fast,
(Walk fast.)
I can walk slow,
(Lumber back and forth.)
And I can stand on one foot just so.
(Stand on one foot.)

I Asked My Mother *(Anonymous)*

I asked my mother for fifty cents,
To see the elephant jump the fence.
He jumped so high that he touched the sky,
And he never came back till the Fourth of July.

I Caught a Fish Alive (Traditional)

One, two, three, four, five,
(Hold up five fingers, one at a time.)
I caught a fish alive.
(Imitate holding up fish.)
Six, seven, eight, nine, ten,
(Raise up fingers of other hand.)
I let it go again.
(Imitate throwing fish back.)
Why did I let it go?
(Hold up hands, looking puzzled.)
Because it bit my finger so!
(Shake right hand.)
Which finger did it bite?
(Hold up right hand.)
The little finger on the right.
(Hold up little finger.)

I Eat My Peas with Honey (Anonymous)

I eat my peas with honey;
I've done it all my life.
It makes the peas taste funny,
But it keeps them on the knife.

If All the World Were Paper
(Nursery Rhyme)

If all the world were paper,
And all the seas were ink,
If all the trees were bread and cheese,
What should we have to drink?
It's enough to make a man like me
Scratch his head and think.

If I Were a Horse (Traditional)

If I were a horse, I'd neigh, of course.
(Hold up two fingers for horse ears at head.)
If I were a bug, I'd curl up in a rug.
(Curl self up into ball.)
If I were a bear, I'd comb my hair.
(Imitate combing body with fingers.)
If I were a pig, I'd dance a jig.
(Dance in place.)
If I were a hen, I'd scratch in my pen.
(Scratch with feet on ground.)
If I were a lynx, I'd sit like a sphinx.
(Hold arms out and close eyes.)
If I were a snail, I'd crawl on the trail.
(Crawl fingers up other arm.)
But if I were a gnu, I'd have nothing to do.
(Sit down, shrugging shoulders, hands up.)

If You Are Happy and You Know It
(Traditional)

If you are happy and you know it, clap your
  hands. (clap, clap)
If you are happy and you know it, clap your
  hands. (clap, clap)
If you are happy and you know it, then your
  face will surely show it.
If you are happy and you know it, clap your
  hands. (clap, clap)

(Repeat song with "stamp your feet," "tap your
head," etc. Each time repeat the previous motions
and add the new one. See how many you can
remember in order.)

I Have Ten Little Fingers (Traditional)

I have ten little fingers,
Ten little toes,
Two little arms,
And one little nose.
One little mouth,
And two little ears,
Two little eyes,
For smiles and tears.
One little head,
And two little feet,
One little chin,
That's me complete!

(Point to body parts as appropriate.)

I Love Little Pussy (Nursery Rhyme)

I love little pussy, her coat is so warm,
And if I don't hurt her, she'll do me no harm.
So I'll not pull her tail nor drive her away,
But pussy and I very gently will play.
She shall sit by my side, and I'll give her some
  food.
And pussy will love me because I am good.

I Love the Mountains (Folk Song)

I love the mountains, I love the rolling hills.
I love the flowers, I love the daffodils.
I love the fireside (clap, clap) when all the lights
  are low.
Dumdiddy, dumdiddy, dumdiddy, dumdiddy.

I Love You (Anonymous)

I love you, I love you,
I love you divine.
Please give me your bubble gum;
You're sitting on mine!

I'm a Little Teapot (Nursery Rhyme)

I'm a little teapot short and stout.
Here is my handle.
(Put hand on hip for handle.)
And here is my spout.
(Turn arm for handle.)
When I get all steamed up, I shall shout,
"Tip me over and pour me out!"
(Tip body over, imitate a pouring teapot.)

I'm a Nut (Traditional)

I'm an acorn, small and round,
Lying on the cold, cold ground.
People pass and step on me,
That's why I'm all cracked, you see.
I'm a nut *(clap, clap).*
I'm a nut *(clap, clap).*
I'm a nut *(clap, clap).*
I'm a nut *(clap, clap).*

I'm Glad (Anonymous)

I'm glad the sky is painted blue,
And the earth is painted green,
With such a lot of nice fresh air
All sandwiched in between.

In a Cabin (Traditional)

In a cabin in a wood, a little man by the window
  stood,
Saw a rabbit hopping by knocking on his door.
"Help me! Help me, sir!" he said, "or the hunters
  will shoot me dead."
"Come little rabbit, come inside, safely you can
  hide."

I Saw Three Ships (Traditional)

I saw three ships come sailing in,
On New Year's Day, on New Year's Day.
I saw three ships come sailing in,
On New Year's Day in the morning.

I Touch (Adapted)

Touch your nose, touch your chin,
Now our game it will begin.
Touch your eyes, touch your knees,
Now pretend you're going to sneeze.
Touch your ears, touch your hair,
Wave your fingers in the air.
Hands on hips, at the waist do bend,
Sit on the floor, and this game will end.

(Imitate designated movements.)

It's Raining, It's Pouring (Traditional)

It's raining, it's pouring, the old man is snoring.
He bumped his head and he went to bed
And he couldn't get up in the morning.
Rain, rain, go away, come again another day.

I've Been Working on the Railroad
(Traditional)

I've been working on the railroad all my live-
  long days.
I've been working on the railroad just a-passing
  time away.
Can't you hear the whistle blowing?
Rise up early in the morn?
Can't you hear the captain shouting,
"Dinah, blow your horn"?

Dinah, won't you blow?
Dinah, won't you blow?
Dinah, won't you blow your ho-o-orn?
Dinah, won't you blow?
Dinah, won't you blow?
Dinah, won't you blow your horn?

Someone's in the kitchen with Dinah.
Someone's in the kitchen, I kno-o-ow!
Someone's in the kitchen with Dinah,
Strummin' on the old banjo and singing,
"Fe-fi-fiddly-i-o,
Fe-fi-fiddly-i-o-o-o,
Fe-fi-fiddly-i-o!"
Strummin' on the old banjo!

Jack Be Nimble (Nursery Rhyme)

Jack be nimble, Jack be quick,
Jack jump over the candlestick.

(Imitate jumping.)

Jack-in-the-Box (Traditional)

Jack-in-the-box all closed up tight, not any air,
  not any light.
(Squat with body in small ball.)
My, but it's dark down here in a heap. Let's
  open the lip,
And up we'll leap!
(Jump up to standing position.)

Jack-o'-Lantern (Traditional)

I'm sometimes big,
(*Arms in circle overhead.*)
I'm sometimes small,
(*Hands form small circle.*)
But always round and yellow.
(*Hands form medium circle.*)
When children fix my famous grin,
(*Smile and point to lips.*)
Then I'm a scary fellow.
(*Make a scary face.*)

Jack Spratt (Nursery Rhyme)

Jack Spratt could eat no fat;
His wife could eat no lean.
And so between them both, you see,
They licked the platter clean.

Jelly (Unknown)

Jelly on my head,
Jelly on my toes,
Jelly on my coat,
Jelly on my nose.

Laughing and a-licking,
Having me a time,
Jelly on my belly,
But I like it fine.

Jelly is my favorite food,
And when I'm in a jelly mood,
I can't ever get enough
Of that yummy, gummy stuff.

Pretty soon it will be spring,
And I'll do my gardening,
But I'll plant no flowerbed;
I'll plant jelly beans instead.

Jingle Bells (Piernot)

Jingle bells, jingle bells,
Jingle all the way.
Oh, what fun it is to ride
In a one-horse open sleigh—hey!

Jingle bells, jingle bells,
Jingle all the way.
Oh, what fun it is to ride
In a one-horse open sleigh.

Dashing through the snow
In a one-horse open sleigh,
O'er the hills we go,
Laughing all the way. Ho, Ho, Ho!

Bells on bobtails ring,
Making spirits bright.
What fun it is to ride and sing
A sleighing song tonight.
O . . . (*Repeat.*)

Johnny Pounds with One Hammer (Traditional)

Johnny pounds with one hammer, one hammer,
  one hammer.
Johnny pounds with one hammer then he
  pounds with two.

Johnny pounds with two hammers, two
  hammers, two hammers.
Johnny pounds with two hammers then he
  pounds with three.

Three . . .

Four . . .

Five . . . Then he goes to sleep.

(*Imitate pounding; in last verse imatates
sleeping*

The Kangaroo (Anonymous)

Old Jumpety-Bumpety-Hop-and-Go-One
Was lying asleep on his side in the sun.
This old kangaroo, he was whisking the flies
With his long glossy tail from his ears and his
  eyes,
Was lying asleep on his side in the sun
Jumpety-Bumpety-Hop-and-Go-One.

A Kite (Anonymous)

I often sit and wish that I
Could be a kite up in the sky,
And ride upon the breeze and go
Whichever way I chanced to blow.

Kitten Is Hiding (Traditional)

A kitten is hiding under a chair,
(*Hide one thumb under other hand.*)
I looked and looked for her everywhere,
(*Hand across eyebrows, looking.*)
Under the table and under the bed;
(*Keep looking around.*)
I looked in the corner, and when I said,
"Come, Kitty, come Kitty, here's milk for you,"
(*Hold out cupped hands.*)
Kitty came running and calling "Mew, Mew."
(*Run fingers of one hand up other arm.*)

Knock at the Door (Traditional)

Knock at the door,
(Tap forehead.)
Peep in.
(Point to eyes.)
Lift the latch,
(Tap end of nose.)
Walk in.
(Open mouth, finger walking towards mouth.)

Kum Ba Ya (Traditional)

Kum ba ya, Lord, kum ba ya,
Kum ba ya, Lord, kum ba ya,
Kum ba ya, Lord, kum ba ya,
Oh, Lord, kum ba ya.
Someone's crying, Lord, kum ba ya . . .
Someone's laughing, Lord . . .
Someone's singing . . .

Lavender's Blue (Nursery Rhyme)

Lavender's blue, diddle, diddle.
Lavender's green.
When I am king, diddle, diddle,
You shall be queen.

Who told you so, diddle, diddle?
Who told you so?
'Twas mine own heart, diddle, diddle,
That told me so.

Roses are red, diddle, diddle.
Violets are blue.
Because you love me, diddle, diddle,
I will love you.

Lazy Mary, Will You Get Up?

(Nursery Rhyme)

Lazy Mary, will you get up,
Will you get up, will you get up?
Lazy Mary, will you get up,
Will you get up today?

No, no, Mother, I won't get up,
I won't get up, I won't get up.
No, no, Mother, I won't get up,
I won't get up today!

Leaves (Traditional)

The leaves are whirling round and round.
(Wave fingers in air.)
The leaves are falling to the ground,
(Wave fingers down to floor.)
Round and round, round and round,
(Roll one hand over the other.)
Falling softly to the ground.
(Softly wave hands down to ground.)

Left to the Window (Traditional)

Left to the window,
(Hands march to the left.)
Right to the door,
(Hands march right.)
Up to the ceiling,
(Point to ceiling.)
Down to the floor.
(Touch floor.)

Let Everyone Clap Hands with Me

(Traditional)

Let everyone clap hands with me. *(clap, clap)*
It's easy as easy can be. *(clap, clap)*
Come on in and join in the game. *(clap, clap)*
Just watch me and you do the same. *(clap, clap)*
Clap hands, clap and be merry,
Clap hands, clap them again.
Clap hands, clap and be merry,
Clap till the walls start to shake, *(clap, clap)*
Clap till the walls start to shake. *(clap, clap)*

Let everyone stomp feet with me. *(stomp, stomp)* . . .

Let everyone slap knees with me. *(slap, slap)* . . .

Let everyone shout out "Yoo-hoo." *("Yoo-hoo!")* . . .

Let everyone whisper "Yoo-hoo." *("yoo-hoo")* . . .

Let Your Hands Go Clap (Adapted)

Let your hands go clap, clap, clap.
(Clap hands.)
Let your fingers tap, tap, tap.
(Tap fingers.)
Roll your hands around and 'round.
(Roll hands one over the other.)
And lay them quietly right down.
(Lay hands in lap.)

Listening Time (Traditional)

Sometimes my hands are at my side;
Then behind my back they hide.
Sometimes I wiggle fingers so,
Shake them fast, shake them slow.
Sometimes my hands go clap, clap, clap;
Then I rest them in my lap.
Now they're quiet as can be.
Because it's listening time, you see!

(Imitate designated movements.)

Little Bo-Peep (Nursery Rhyme)

Little Bo-Peep has lost her sheep
And doesn't know where to find them.
Leave them alone and they will come home,
Wagging their tails behind them.

Little Boy Blue (Nursery Rhyme)

Little Boy Blue, come blow your horn,
The sheep's in the meadow, the cow's in the
corn.
Where is the boy who looks after the sheep?
He's under the haystack, fast asleep.

Little Bunny Foo Foo (Traditional)

Little Bunny Foo Foo,
Hopping through the forest,
(Raise two fingers and "hop" hand through air.)
Scooping up the field mice
(Scoop cupped hand in air.)
And popping them on the head!
("Pop" fist of one hand in palm of other hand.)
Down came the good fairy and said,
"Little Bunny Foo Foo,
I don't like your attitude—
(Shake a finger as if scolding Bunny.)
Scooping up the field mice
(Scoop cupped hand in air.)
And popping them on the head.
("Pop" fist of one hand in palm of other hand.)
I'll give you three chances
And if you don't behave,
(Shake a finger as if scolding Bunny.)
I'll turn you into a GOON!"

And the next day came
Little Bunny Foo Foo,
Hopping through the forest . . .
*(Repeat as above for "two chances" and "one
more chance.")*

And on the fourth day came
Little Bunny Foo Foo, . . .
Down came the good fairy for the last time and
said,
"Little Bunny Foo Foo,
I gave you three chances
And you still didn't behave.
(Shake a finger as if scolding Bunny.)
Now I'll turn you into a GOON!"
POOF!
(Hold up both fists and quickly open them.)

*(Young children enjoy this song for its motions
even though they may not understand its moral:
Hare today and goon tomorrow.)*

Little Drops of Water (Traditional)

Little drops of water,
Little grains of sand
Make the mighty ocean
And the pleasant land.

Little Jack Horner (Nursery Rhyme)

Little Jack Horner sat in a corner,
Eating his Christmas pie.
He stuck in his thumb and pulled out a plum,
And said, "What a fine boy am I."

Little Liza Jane (Folk Song)

You got a gal and I got none, Li'l Liza Jane.
Come my love and be my one, Li'l Liza Jane.
O, Eliza, Li'l Liza Jane.
O, Eliza, Li'l Liza Jane.

(Wave arms on "O, Eliza.")

Little Miss Muffet (Nursery Rhyme)

Little Miss Muffet sat on a tuffet, eating her
curds and whey.
Along came a spider and sat down beside her,
And frightened Miss Muffet away.

Little Mouse (Traditional)

See the little mousie creeping up the stair,
(Creep fingers of one hand up other arm.)
Looking for a warm nest. There, oh, there!
(Snuggle fingers into crease at elbow.)

Little Nut Tree (Traditional)

I had a little nut tree, nothing would it bear
But a silver nutmeg and a golden pear.
The King of Spain's daughter came to visit me,
And all for the sake of my little nut tree.

Little Peter Rabbit (Adapted)

Little Peter Rabbit had a fly upon his ear.
Little Peter Rabbit had a fly upon his ear.
Little Peter Rabbit had a fly upon his ear,
And he flicked it 'til it flew away.

Little Peter *(make rabbit-ears motion instead of
saying "rabbit")* had a fly upon his ear.
Little Peter *(rabbit motion)* had a fly upon his
ear.
Little Peter *(rabbit motion)* had a fly upon his
ear,
And he flicked it 'til it flew away.

*(Continue song, substituting motions for words:
waving arms for "fly," touching ear for "ear,"
flicking arms for "flicked," and waving arms for
"flew away.")*

Resources for Every Day in Every Way

Little Sally Saucer *(Traditional)*

Little Sally Saucer, sitting in the water.
Weeping and crying.
Cry, Sally, cry.
Wipe out your eyes.
Turn to the east
And turn to the west.
Turn to the one that you love best!

(Children stand holding hands in a circle with one child in the center. With eyes closed, the child turns and points to the "one loved best.")

Little Tom Tinker *(Nursery Rhyme)*

Little Tom Tinker got burned with a clinker,
And he began to cry, "Mama, Mama!
What a poor fellow am I!"

Little Tom Tucker *(Nursery Rhyme)*

Little Tom Tucker sings for his supper,
What shall he sing for? White bread and butter.
How shall he cut it without any knife?
How shall he marry without any wife?

London Bridge *(Nursery Rhyme)*

London bridge is falling down, falling down,
 falling down.
London bridge is falling down, my fair lady.
*(Two children hold hands to form a bridge for
 the others to pass under.)*

Take the keys and lock her up, lock her up, lock
 her up.
Take the keys and lock her up, my fair lady.
*(Children forming the bridge "capture" one of
 the children in the bridge.)*

Long, Long Ago *(Traditional)*

Tell me the tales that to me were so dear
Long, long ago; long, long ago.
Sing me the songs I delighted to hear
Long, long ago, long ago.

Looby Loo *(Traditional)*

Here we go looby loo,
Here we go looby light,
Here we go looby loo,
All on a Saturday night.
You put your right hand in, you put your right
 hand out,
You give your right hand a shake, shake,
 shake,
And turn yourself about!

You put your left hand in . . .

You put your right foot . . .

You put your left foot . . .

You put your whole self . . .

*(Children join hands in a circle and skip to the
center and back, then follow directions in song.)*

Love Somebody, Yes I Do *(Folk Song)*

Love somebody, yes, I do,
Love somebody, yes, I do,
Love somebody, yes, I do,
Love somebody, but I won't tell who.

Love my Daddy, yes, I do . . .

Love my Mommy, yes, I do . . .

Love my Gramma, yes, I do . . .

Love my Granpa, yes, I do . . .

Mabel, Mabel *(Traditional)*

Mabel, Mabel, set the table,
Don't forget the salt and pepper.

*(Slap thighs, clap hands, slap partner's hands,
one at a time. Repeat rhyme faster each time.)*

Make New Friends *(Traditional)*

Make new friends but keep the old.
One is silver and the other's gold.

*(Divide the class into two groups and sing in a
round.)*

Mary Had a Little Lamb
(Nursery Rhyme)

Mary had a little lamb, little lamb, little lamb.
Mary had a little lamb. Its fleece was white as
snow.

Everywhere that Mary went, Mary went, Mary
went,
Everywhere that Mary went the lamb was sure
to go.

It followed her to school one day, school one
day, school one day.
It followed her to school one day, which was
against the rules.

It made the children laugh and play, laugh and
play, laugh and play.
It made the children laugh and play to see a
lamb in school.

Mary Mack *(Traditional)*

Miss Mary Mack, Mack, Mack.
All dressed in black, black, black.
With silver buttons, buttons, buttons
Up and down her back, back, back.
She asked her mother, mother, mother
For fifty cents, cents, cents
To see the elephants, elephants, elephants
Jump off the fence, fence, fence.
They jumped so high, high, high
They touched the sky, sky, sky
And they never came back, back, back,
'til the fourth of July, July, July.

*(Children can clap hands or strike palms with a
partner during this song.)*

Mary Wore Her Red Dress *(Folk Song)*

Mary wore her red dress, red dress, red dress.
Mary wore her red dress all day long.

Mary wore her black hat . . .

Mary wore her blue shoes . . .

Mary wore her green socks . . .

(Repeat, adding clothing items.)

Merrily We Roll Along *(Traditional)*

(Tune: "Mary Had a Little Lamb")

Merrily we roll along, roll along, roll along.
Merrily we roll along, o'er the deep blue sea.

Michael Finnegan *(Traditional Irish)*

There was a young man named Michael
Finnegan,
He grew whiskers on his chinnegan,
The wind came up and blew them in again,
Poor, poor Michael Finnegan, Begin again!

Michael, Row the Boat Ashore
(Spiritual)

Michael, row the boat ashore, Hallelujah!
Michael, row the boat ashore, Hallelujah!
Sister, help to trim the sails, Hallelujah!
Sister, help to trim the sails, Hallelujah!
The river is deep and the river is wide,
Hallelujah!
Milk and honey on the other side, Hallelujah!

(Repeat.)

Mistress Mary, Quite Contrary
(Traditional)

Mistress Mary, quite contrary,
How does your garden grow?
With silver bells and cockleshells
And pretty maids all in a row.

The More We Get Together *(Traditional)*

(Tune: "Did You Ever See a Lassie?")

The more we get together, together, together,
The more we get together, the happier we'll be,
'Cause your friends are my friends,
And my friends are your friends.
The more we get together,
The happier we'll be.

The Muffin Man *(Nursery Rhyme)*

Oh, do you know the muffin man, the muffin
man, the muffin man?
Oh, do you know the muffin man who lives on
Drury Lane?

Oh, yes I know the muffin man, the muffin man,
the muffin man.
Oh, yes I know the muffin man who lives on
Drury Lane.

Mulberry Bush: Version One
(Traditional)

Here we go 'round the mulberry bush,
The mulberry bush, the mulberry bush.
Here we go 'round the mulberry bush
So early in the morning.

*(Sing and act out motions for the following
verses.)*
This is the way we wash our face,
Wash our face, wash our face,
This is the way we wash our face
So early in the morning.

This is the way we make our bed . . .

This is the way we brush our teeth . . .

This is the way we comb our hair . . .

This is the way we tie our shoes . . .

(Add other verses.)

Mulberry Bush: Version Two
(Traditional)

Here we go 'round the mulberry bush,
The mulberry bush, the mulberry bush.
Here we go 'round the mulberry bush
So early in the morning.

(Sing and act out the following verses.)
This is the way we wash the clothes,
Wash the clothes, wash the clothes.
This is the way we wash the clothes,
So early in the morning.

This is the way we dry the clothes . . .

This is the way we iron the clothes . . .

This is the way we put on our clothes . . .

*(Add other verses and imitate designated
motions.)*

Mulberry Bush: Version Three
(Traditional)

Here we go 'round the mulberry bush,
The mulberry bush, the mulberry bush.
Here we go 'round the mulberry bush
So early in the morning.

This is the way we put out the fire . . .

This is the way we direct the traffic . . .

This is the way we bake the bread . . .

*(Each child designates a community helper to
imitate.)*

My Bicycle *(Adapted)*

One wheel, two wheels, on the ground.
(Form circles with hands.)
My feet push the pedals 'round and 'round.
(Roll one hand over the other.)
My hands upon the bar to steer,
(Imitate holding handlebars.)
Watch out, I'm coming, everyone clear!
(Imitate driving bicycle.)

My Bonnie *(Traditional)*

My Bonnie lies over the ocean.
My Bonnie lies over the sea.
My Bonnie lies over the ocean.
Oh, bring back my Bonnie to me.
Bring back, bring back,
Oh, bring back my Bonnie to me, to me.
Bring back, bring back,
Oh, bring back my Bonnie to me.

My Dreydl *(Words by S. S. Grossman)*

I have a little dreydl.
I made it out of clay.
And when it's dry and ready,
Then dreydl I shall play.
Oh, dreydl, dreydl, dreydl,
I made it out of clay.
Oh, dreydl, dreydl, dreydl,
Now ready I shall play.

(Reprinted from The Songs We Sing, *selected
and edited by Harry Coopersmith, copyright 1950
by the United Synagogue of America, with
permission by The United Synagogue of America
Commission on Jewish Education.)*

My Father Owns the Butcher Shop
(Anonymous)

My father owns the butcher shop.
My mother cuts the meat.
And I'm the little hot dog
That runs around the street.

My Garden *(Traditional)*

This is my garden. I'll rake it with care,
(Imitate raking.)
And then some flower seeds I'll plant in there.
(Imitate planting seeds.)
The sun will shine,
(Make circle above head with hands.)
And the rain will fall,
(Fingers flutter, imitating rain.)
And my garden will blossom and grow straight
  and tall.
(Imitate flowers blooming with hands.)

My Hands *(Traditional)*

My hands upon my head I place,
On my shoulders, on my face.
Now I raise them up so high,
Make my fingers quickly fly.
Now I clap them, one, two, three.
Then I fold them silently.

(Imitate directions.)

My Name *(Adapted)*

(Tune: "Mary Had a Little Lamb")

_____is my name, is my name, is
  my name.
_____is my name, what is your
  name?

(Sing around a circle.)

My Tall Silk Hat *(Traditional)*

One day I took a ride upon the subway,
My tall silk hat, my tall silk hat!
I went to put it on the seat beside me
My tall silk hat, my tall silk hat!
A big fat lady came and sat upon it,
My tall silk hat, she squashed it flat!
And then a big fat lady sat upon it,
My tall silk hat, it looked like that!
Christopher Columbus, now what do you think
  of that?
A big fat lady sat upon my hat!
Upon my hat, upon my hat,
Oh yes, she sat upon my hat!
Christopher Columbus, now what do you think
  of that?

(Imitate appropriate movements.)

My Turtle *(Traditional)*

This is my turtle. He lives in a shell.
*(Put one hand over the other, wiggle extended t
  thumb.)*
He likes his home very well.
(Pull thumb in and extend it again.)
He pokes his head out when he wants to eat.
(Extend thumb.)
And pulls it back when he wants to sleep.
(Pull thumb back under hand.)

Noble Duke of York *(Traditional)*

The noble Duke of York, he had ten thousand
  men.
He marched them up to the top of the hill
And marched them down again.

And when you're up, you're up,
And when you're down, you're down,
And when you're only halfway up,
You're neither up nor down!

*(Children form two lines facing partners. They
march to partner on first verse and hold hands.
On second verse they imitate stretching up,
squatting down, and standing halfway up. Repeat
first verse, marching back to place in line.)*

The North Wind Doth Blow *(Traditional)*

The north wind doth blow,
And we shall have snow.
And what will the robin do then, poor thing?
He'll sit in the barn and keep himself warm,
And hide his head under his wing, poor thing!

Oats, Peas, Beans *(Traditional)*

Oats, peas, beans, and barley grow.
Oats, peas, beans, and barley grow.
Do you or I or anyone know
How oats, peas, beans, and barley grow?
*(Children join hands and skip around in a
circle.)*

First the farmer sows his seeds.
Then he stands and takes his ease,
Stamps his feet, and claps his hand;
And turns around to view his land.
*(One child, the farmer, stands in the middle and
acts out the words.)*

Waiting for a partner,
Waiting for a partner,
Open the ring and take one in,
And then we'll dance and gaily sing.
*(Farmer chooses a partner to dance inside the
  circle as the others skip in a circle.)*

O Christmas Tree (German Folk Song)

O Christmas tree, O Christmas tree,
How evergreen your branches.
(Repeat.)

You never change the whole year 'round,
You brighten up the snowy ground.
O Christmas tree, O Christmas tree,
How evergreen your branches.

(Children may substitute "O Tannenbaum" for
"O Christmas tree.")

Oh Dear, What Can the Matter Be?
(Traditional)

Oh dear, what can the matter be?
Oh dear, what can the matter be?
Oh dear, what can the matter be?
Johnny's too long at the fair.

He promised to bring me a basket of posies,
A garland of lilies, a garland of roses.
He promised to bring me a bunch of blue
  ribbons
To tie up my bonnie brown hair.

Oh dear, what can the matter be?
Oh dear, what can the matter be?
Oh dear, what can the matter be?
Johnny's too long at the fair.

Oh How Lovely Is the Evening
(Traditional)

Oh, how lovely is the evening, is the evening,
When the bells are sweetly ringing, sweetly
  ringing,
Ding, dong, ding, dong, ding, dong.

Oh Where Has My Little Dog Gone?
(Traditional)

Oh where, oh where has my little dog gone?
Oh where, oh where can he be?
With his ears cut short and his tail cut long,
Oh where, oh where can he be?

The Old Gray Cat (Traditional)

The old gray cat is sleeping, sleeping, sleeping,
The old gray cat is sleeping in the house.

The little mice come creeping, creeping,
  creeping,
The little mice come creeping in the house.

The little mice are nibbling . . .

The old gray cat comes sneaking . . .

The little mice all scamper . . . from the house!

(Imitate appropriate motions of sleeping,
creeping, nibbling, sneaking, and scampering for
each verse.)

Old King Cole (Nursery Rhyme)

Old King Cole was a merry old soul and a
  merry old soul was he.
He called for his pipe and he called for his bowl
And he called for his fiddlers three.
Now every fiddler, he had a fiddle and a very
  fine fiddle had he.
Oh there's none so rare as can compare,
With King Cole and his fiddlers three.

Old MacDonald (Traditional)*

Old MacDonald had a farm. E-I-E-I-O.
And on his farm he had a cow. E-I-E-I-O.
With a moo-moo here and a moo-moo there.
Here a moo, there a moo, everywhere a moo-
  moo.
Old MacDonald had a farm. E-I-E-I-O.

Old MacDonald had a farm. E-I-E-I-O.
And on his farm he had a duck. E-I-E-I-O.
With a quack-quack here and a quack-quack
  there.
Here a quack, there a quack, everywhere a
  quack-quack,
A moo-moo here and a moo-moo there,
Here a moo, there a moo, everywhere a moo-
  moo.
Old MacDonald had a farm. E-I-E-I-O.

(Repeat with pig—oink, horse—heeeeee,
chicken—cluck, and other favorite animals.)

Old Mother Hubbard (Nursery Rhyme)

Old Mother Hubbard went to the cupboard,
To fetch her poor doggie a bone.
But when she got there, the cupboard was
  bare,
And so the poor doggie had none.

Old Woman and the Pig (Folk Song)

There was an old woman and she had a little
  pig, oink, oink, oink.
There was an old woman and she had a little
  pig.
He didn't cost much 'cause he wasn't very big,
  oink, oink, oink.

One Finger, One Thumb, Keep Moving
(Traditional)

One finger, one thumb, keep moving.
One finger, one thumb, one hand, keep moving.
One finger, one thumb, one hand, one arm,
  keep moving.
One finger, one thumb, one hand, one arm, one
  foot, keep moving.

(Add motions as designated in song.)

One for the Money (Traditional)

One for the money.
Two for the show.
Three to get ready.
And four to go!

(Hold up designated number of fingers.)

One Little Elephant (Traditional)

One little elephant went out to play,
Out on a spider's web one day.
He had such enormous fun
That he called for another little elephant
  to come.

Two little elephants went out to play . . .

Three little elephants . . .

(Continue to desired number.)

One Misty, Moisty Morning
(Anonymous)

One misty, moisty morning,
When cloudy was the weather,
I chanced to meet an old man
Clothed all in leather.
He began to compliment
And I began to grin.
How do you do? And how do you do?
And how do you do again?

One Potato, Two Potato (Traditional)

One potato, two potato, three potato, four,
Five potato, six potato, seven potato, more.

(Children put fists together in a circle. The
teacher goes around tapping each fist to the
song, and the child whose fist is tapped on "more"
has his or her fist eliminated. The last fist to
remain is a "hot potato.")

One, Two, Buckle My Shoe
(Nursery Rhyme)

One, two, buckle my shoe.
Three, four, shut the door.
Five, six, pick up sticks.
Seven, eight, lay them straight.
Nine, ten, a big fat hen.

(Imitate designated motions.)

One, Two, Three Little Witches
(Traditional)

(Tune: "Ten Little Indians")

One little, two little, three little witches
(Hold up three fingers.)
Fly over haystacks, fly over ditches,
(Imitate flying.)
Slide down moonbeams without any hitches,
(Slide hand downward.)
Heigh-ho! Halloween's here!
(Clap hands.)

Open Them, Shut Them (Traditional)

Open them, shut them, open them, shut them,
(Open and close hands.)
Give a little clap, clap, clap.
(Clap hands.)
Open them, shut them, open them, shut them,
(Open and close hands.)
Put them in your lap, lap, lap.
(Set hands in lap.)
Creep them, creep them, creep them, creep
  them,
(Creep hand up other arm.)
Right up to your chin, chin, chin.
(Tap chin.)
Open up your little mouth but do not let them in,
  in, in!
(Open mouth, touch outside of mouth.)

Over in the Meadow (Traditional)

Over in the meadow, in the sand, in the sun,
Lived an old mother frog and her little froggie
  one.
"Croak," said the mother. "I croak," said the
  one,
So they croaked and they croaked in the sand
  in the sun.

Over in the meadow, in the stream so blue,
Lived an old mother fish and her little fishes
  two.
"Swim," said the mother. "We swim," said the
  two,
So they swam and they swam in the stream so
  blue.

Over in the meadow, on the branch of the tree,
Lived an old mother bird and her little birdies
  three.
"Sing," said the mother. "We sing," said the
  three,
So they sang and they sang on a branch of the
  tree.

Over the River and Through the Woods
(Traditional)

Over the river and through the woods
To grandmother's house we go.
The horse knows the way to carry the sleigh
Through the wild and wintery snow-o!

Over the river and through the woods
Oh, how the wind does blow.
It stings your nose and bites your toes
As over the ground we go.

Paper of Pins (Folk Song)

(Proposal verse.)
I'll give to you a paper of pins,
And that's the way my love begins,
If you will marry me, me, me,
If you will marry me.

(Rejection verse.)
I'll not accept your paper of pins,
If that's the way your love begins,
And I'll not marry you, you, you,
And I'll not marry you!

(Acceptance verse.)
Yes, I'll accept your paper of pins,
If that's the way your love begins,
And I will marry you, you, you,
Yes, I will marry you.

(Take turns singing the verses—girls courting
boys, and boys courting girls—with acceptance
and rejection replies.)

Pat-A-Cake (Nursery Rhyme)

Pat-a-cake, pat-a-cake, baker's man,
(Clap hands.)
Bake me a cake just as fast as you can.
(Clap hands.)
Pat it and shape it and mark it with a B,
(Pat, mold, and mark hand with other.)
And put it in the oven for baby and me.
(Imitate putting in oven, then point away and
  to self.)

Paw-paw Patch (Folk Song)

Where, oh where is sweet little Susie?
Where, oh where is sweet little Susie?
Where, oh where is sweet little Susie?
Way down yonder in the paw-paw patch.

Come on, boys, let's go find her.
Come on, boys, let's go find her.
Come on, boys, let's go find her
Way down yonder in the paw-paw patch.

Peanut Butter (Traditional)

Peanut, peanut butter, (Whisper "Jelly.")
Peanut, peanut butter, (Whisper "Jelly.")
First you take the peanuts and you smash 'em,
  you smash 'em,
You smash 'em, smash 'em, smash 'em.
(Imitate smashing peanuts.)
Then you take the peanut butter and you
  spread it, you spread it,
You spread it, spread it, spread it.
(Imitate spreading peanut butter.)

Peanut, peanut butter, (Whisper "Jelly.")
Peanut, peanut butter, (Whisper "Jelly.")
Then you take the grapes and you squish 'em,
You squish 'em, you squish 'em, squish 'em,
  squish 'em.
(Imitate squishing.)
And then you take the jelly and you spread it,
You spread it, you spread it, spread it,
  spread it.
(Imitate spreading.)

Peanut, peanut butter, (Whisper "Jelly.")
Peanut, peanut butter, (Whisper "Jelly.")
Then you put the bread together and you cut it,
You cut it, you cut it, cut it, cut it.
(Imitate cutting.)

Then you munch it, you munch it,
You munch it, munch it, munch it.
(Imitate chewing and swallowing.)

Peanut, peanut butter, *(Whisper "Jelly.")*
Peanut, peanut butter, *(Whisper "Jelly.")*

Pease Porridge Hot *(Nursery Rhyme)*

Pease porridge hot, pease porridge cold,
Pease porridge in the pot nine days old.
Some like it hot, and some like it cold.
I like it in the pot nine days old!

Phone Number Song *(Adapted)*

(TUNE: "TWINKLE, TWINKLE LITTLE STAR")

8-4-6-8-1-2-6,
8-4-6-8-1-2-6,
8-4-6-8-1-2-6,
8-4-6-8-1-2-6,
8-4-6-8-1-2-6.
Sing my number, sing it quick.

(Use any seven-digit number with this song.)

Pitter-pat *(Anonymous)*

Pitter-pat, pitter-pat,
Oh so many hours.
Although it keeps me in the house,
It's very good for flowers.

Playmates *(Cynthia Holley)*

(TUNE: "ONE LITTLE ELEPHANT")

One little girl went out to play,
On a warm and sunny summer day.
Along came a friend so happy and gay,
She joined that girl and decided to stay.

Two little playmates wanted to run,
So they romped in the grass and had so much
  fun.
Another little boy came along with his gun.
Now three little playmates sat down in the sun.

Three little playmates opened up a store,
Along came a customer and that made four.
These four friends heard a knock on the door,
But when they answered they said, "No more!"

Police Officer *(Traditional)*

Police officers are helpers wherever they may
  stand.
(Stand with feet apart, hands at hips.)
They tell us when to stop and go by holding up
  their hands.
*(Signal stop by holding up hand and go by
  pointing index finger.)*

Polly Put the Kettle On *(Nursery Rhyme)*

Polly put the kettle on, Polly put the kettle on,
Polly put the kettle on, we'll all have tea.
Sukey take it off again, Sukey take it off again,
Sukey take it off again, they've all gone home.

Polly Wolly Doodle *(Folk Song)*

Oh, I went down South for to see my Sal,
Sing Polly Wolly Doodle all the day.
My Sal she is a spunky gal,
Sing Polly Wolly Doodle all day.
Fare thee well, fare thee well,
Fare thee well my fairy fay,
For I'm goin' to Louisiana,
For to see my Susyanna,
Sing Polly Wolly Doodle all the day.

Pop Goes the Weasel *(Nursery Rhyme)*

All around the cobbler's bench the monkey
  chased the weasel.
The monkey thought 'twas all in fun.
Pop goes the weasel.
(Clap hands on "Pop.")

Pound Goes the Hammer *(Traditional)*

Pound, pound, pound, pound, pound goes the
  hammer,
(Hammer one fist with other, thumb up.)
Pound, pound, pound, pound, pound, pound,
  pound.
Bzz, bzz, bzz, bzz, bzz goes the big saw,
(Imitate sawing.)
Bzz, bzz, bzz, bzz, bzz, bzz, bzz.
Chop, chop, chop, chop, chop goes the big axe,
(Imitate chopping with axe.)
Chop, chop, chop, chop, chop, chop, chop.

Punchinello *(Traditional French)*

What can you do, Punchinello, funny fellow?
What can you do, Punchinello, right now?
We'll do it too, Punchinello.
We'll do it too, right now.

*(Children stand in circle. Child in center creates
a rhythm and others imitate the motion or action.)*

Question *(Anonymous)*

Do you love me,
Or do you not?
You told me once,
But I forgot.

Rag Doll *(Traditional)*

Let's play rag doll; let's not make a sound.
(Finger to lips, "Sh!")
Fling your legs and body loosely around.
(Move body in limp motion.)
Fling your arms and your feet, and let your
head go free,
(Fling arms and feet, dangle head.)
Be the raggiest rag doll you ever did see.
(Flop body loosely.)

Rain on the Green Grass *(Anonymous)*

Rain on the green grass,
And rain on the tree,
And rain on the housetop,
But not upon me!

Rain, Rain, Go Away *(Folk Song)*

Rain, rain, go away.
Come again another day,
Rain, rain, go away.
Little Johnny wants to play.

Ride a Cock Horse *(Nursery Rhyme)*

Ride a cock horse to Banbury Cross
To see a fine lady upon a white horse.
With rings on her fingers and bells on her toes,
She shall have music wherever she goes.

Right Hand, Left Hand *(Traditional)*

This is my right hand, I'll raise it up high.
(Lift hand high over head.)
This is my left hand, I'll touch the sky.
(Raise left hand up overhead.)
Right hand, left hand, roll them round.
(Shake each hand; then roll one over other.)
Left hand, right hand, pound, pound, pound.
*(Show each hand; then pound one fist on
 other.)*

Ring Around the Rosie *(Traditional)*

Ring around the rosie,
A pocket full of posies,
Ashes, ashes, we all fall down.

*(Children hold hands and walk around the circle
singing this tune.)*

Robin Redbreast *(Nursery Rhyme)*

Little Robin Redbreast sat upon a rail,
Niddle, naddle went his head.
Wiggle, waggle went his tail.

(Nod fist for head; wiggle fingers for tail.)

Rock-a-bye Baby *(Traditional)*

Rock-a-bye baby in the treetop.
When the wind blows, the cradle will rock.
When the bough breaks, the cradle will fall
And down will come baby, cradle and all.

A Rocket in My Pocket *(Anonymous)*

I've got a rocket
In my pocket.
I cannot stop to play.
Away it goes!
I've burned my toes.
It's Independence Day.

Roses Are Red *(Anonymous)*

Roses are red.
Violets are blue.
Sugar is sweet,
And so are YOU!

Row, Row, Row Your Boat *(Traditional)*

Row, row, row your boat,
Gently down the stream.
Merrily, merrily, merrily, merrily,
Life is but a dream.

(Divide into two groups and sing as a round.)

Rub-a-Dub-Dub *(Nursery Rhyme)*

Rub-a-dub-dub, three men in a tub,
And who do you think they be?
The butcher, the baker, the candlestick maker,
Turn them out, knaves all three!

Safety Belts *(National Safety Council)*

(Tune: "Jingle Bells")

Safety belts, safety belts, wear them all the
 way,
Every time you're in the car, any night or day—
 oh—
Safety belts, safety belts, put them round your
 lap,
Then before you start to ride, everybody SNAP!

A Sailor Went to Sea, Sea, Sea
(Traditional)

A sailor went to sea, sea, sea,
To see what he could see, see, see,
But all that he could see, see, see,
Was the bottom of the deep blue sea, sea, sea!

(Slap thighs, clap hands, and slap palms of another child for each "sea, sea, sea.")

Sally Go Round the Sun *(Traditional)*

Sally go round the sun,
Sally go round the moon,
Sally go round the chimney pots
Every afternoon. BUMP!

(Children skip in circle, holding hands. On BUMP, they jump up and change directions. Repeat several times.)

Santa *(Traditional)*

Down the chimney dear Santa Claus crept
(Poke index finger into loose fist of other hand.)
Into the room while all the children slept.
(Lay three fingers across palm of other hand.)
He saw their stockings hung in line
(Suspend three fingers in air.)
And filled them with candy and goodies fine.
(Imitate filling stockings.)
Although he counted them—one, two, three—
(Point as if counting to three.)
The baby's stocking he could not see.
(Hand across eyebrows, looking.)
"Ho, ho," said Santa. "That won't do."
(Hold tummy and laugh.)
So he popped her present right into her shoe.
(Cup one hand and put other inside.)

The Sea *(Anonymous)*

Behold the wonders of the mighty deep,
Where crabs and lobsters learn to creep,
And little fishes learn to swim,
And clumsy sailors tumble in.

See-saw, Margery Daw *(Nursery Rhyme)*

See-saw, Margery Daw, Johnny shall have a
new master.
He shall have but a penny a day,
Because he can't work any faster.

Senses *(Headland)*

Little eyes see pretty things.
Little nose smells what is sweet.
Little ears hear pleasant sounds.
Mouth likes luscious things to eat.

(Touch appropriate facial feature.)

She'll Be Coming 'Round the Mountain
(Folk Song)

She'll be coming 'round the mountain when she
comes. Toot, toot!
She'll be coming 'round the mountain when she
comes. Toot, toot!
She'll be coming 'round the mountain, she'll be
coming 'round the mountain,
She'll be coming 'round the mountain when she
comes. Toot, toot!

She'll be driving six white horses when she
comes. Whoa back!
She'll be driving six white horses when she
comes. Whoa back!
She'll be driving six white horses, she'll be
driving six white horses,
She'll be driving six white horses when she
comes. Whoa back!

We'll all go out to meet her when she comes. Hi
babe!
Oh, we'll all go out to meet her when she
comes. Hi babe!
Oh, we'll all go out to meet her, we'll all go out
to meet her,
Oh, we'll all go out to meet her when she
comes. Hi babe!

We'll all eat chicken and dumplings when she
comes. Mmm, Mmm!
We'll all eat chicken and dumplings when she
comes. Mmm, Mmm!
Oh, we'll all eat chicken and dumplings, we'll all
eat chicken and dumplings,
We'll all eat chicken and dumplings when she
comes. Mmm, Mmm!

We'll wear our red pajamas when she comes.
Scratch, scratch.
We'll wear our red pajamas when she comes.
Scratch, scratch.
Oh, we'll wear our red pajamas, we'll wear our
red pajamas,
We'll wear our red pajamas when she comes.
Scratch, scratch.

Shoo Fly (Folk Song)

Shoo fly, don't bother me,
Shoo fly, don't bother me,
Shoo fly, don't bother me,
I belong to somebody.
I feel, I feel, I feel,
I feel like a morning star.
I feel, I feel, I feel,
I feel like a morning star.

Simple Simon (Nursery Rhyme)

Simple Simon met a pieman going to the fair.
Said Simple Simon to the pieman, "Let me taste
your ware."
Said the pieman to Simple Simon, "Show me
first your penny."
Said Simple Simon to the pieman, "Indeed, I
have not any."

Sing a Song of Sixpence

(Nursery Rhyme)

Sing a song of sixpence, a pocket full of rye,
Four and twenty blackbirds baked in a pie;
When the pie was opened, the birds began to
sing.
Wasn't that a dainty dish to set before the king?

The king was in his counting house counting
out his money.
The queen was in the parlor eating bread and
honey.
The maid was in the garden hanging out the
clothes.
Along came a blackbird and snipped off her
nose!

Six Little Ducks (Traditional)

Six little ducks that I once knew,
Fat ones, skinny ones, tall ones too.
(Imitate fat, skinny, and tall with arms.)
But the one little duck with the feather in his
back,
(Hold hand up behind head.)
He led the others with a quack, quack, quack,
A quack, quack, quack, a quack, quack, quack.
He led the others with a quack, quack, quack,
(Hold hands together at palms, quacking.)

Down to the river they would go,
Wibble, wobble, wibble, wobble, to and fro.
*(With hands bent out at sides, wobble back and
forth.)*

And the one little duck . . .

Home from the river they would come,
Wibble, wobble, wibble, wobble, ho, ho, hum.
*(With hands bent out at sides, wobble back and
forth.)*
And the one little duck . . .

Skip to My Lou (Traditional)

Skip, skip, skip to my Lou.
Skip, skip, skip to my Lou.
Skip, skip, skip to my Lou.
Skip to my Lou, my darling.

Fly in the buttermilk, shoo, fly, shoo.
Fly in the buttermilk, shoo, fly, shoo.
Fly in the buttermilk, shoo, fly, shoo.
Skip to my Lou, my darling.

Skip a little faster, this'll never do . . .

Hurry up slow poke, do, do, do . . .

(Add more verses.)

Sleep, Baby, Sleep (German Lullaby)

Sleep, baby, sleep!
Thy father watches the sheep.
Thy mother is shaking the dreamland tree,
And down falls a little dream on thee.
Sleep, baby, sleep!

Sleepy Fingers (Traditional)

My fingers are so sleepy; it's time they went to
bed.
So first you, Baby Finger, tuck in your little
head.
Ring man, now it's your turn, and come, Tall
Man great.
Now Pointer Finger hurry, because it's getting
late.
Let's see if all are snuggled—
No, here's one more to come.
So come, lie close, little brother,
Make room for Master Thumb.

(Point to each finger as appropriate.)

The Snail (Anonymous)

The snail he lives in his hard round house,
In the orchard, under a tree.
Says he, "I have but a single room;
But it's large enough for me."

The snail in his little house doth dwell
All the week from end to end.
You're at home, Master Snail;
That's all very well,
But you never receive a friend.

Snowflakes (Adapted)

Snowflakes whirling all around,
Snowflakes whirling 'round and 'round,
Till they cover all the ground.

(Flutter fingers in air and float down to ground.)

Snowmen (Traditional)*

Five little snowmen standing in a row,
(Hold up five fingers.)
Each with a hat and a great big bow,
(Form hat and bowtie with fingers.)
Five little snowmen dressed for a show,
(Hold up five fingers.)
Now they are ready. Where will they go?
(Put hand across eyebrows, looking.)
Wait till the sun shines; soon they will go
(Hold arms overhead making sunshine.)
Down through the fields with the melting snow.
(Melt arms down to sides.)

Solomon Grundy (Anonymous)

Solomon Grundy,
Born on a Monday,
Christened on Tuesday,
Married on Wednesday,
Took ill on Thursday,
Worse on Friday,
Died on Saturday,
Buried on Sunday.
This is the end
Of Solomon Grundy.

Somebody Loves You (Anonymous)

Somebody loves you deep and true.
If I weren't so bashful, I'd tell you who.

Something About Me (Anonymous)

There's something about me
That I'm knowing.
There's something about me
That isn't showing.
I'm growing!

Spin a Coin (Anonymous)

Spin a coin, spin a coin,
All fall down.
Queen Nefertiti
Stalks through the town.
Over the pavements
Her feet go crack.
Her legs as tall
As a chimney stack.
Her fingers flicker
Like snakes in the air.
The walls split open
At her green-eyed stare.
Her voice is thin
As the ghosts of bees.
She will crumble your bones;
She will make your blood freeze.
Spin a coin, spin a coin,
All fall down.
Queen Nefertiti
Stalks through the town.

Starlight, Star Bright (Traditional)

Starlight, star bright,
First star I see tonight,
Wish I may, wish I might
Have the wish I wish tonight.

Stop, Look, and Listen (Traditional)

Stop, look, and listen when you cross the
  street.
(Stand tall.)
First use your eyes, then use your ears,
(Point to body parts.)
And then you use your feet.
(Imitate walking.)

Swing Them (Traditional)

Swing them, swing them, oh so high.
Let them like the birdies fly.
Flutter, flutter to the ground.
Pick them up and twirl them around.

(Imitate respective movements.)

Swinging (Traditional)

Hold on tightly as we go,
Swinging high and swinging low.

(Imitate swinging, with clasped hands swaying back and forth.)

Tall and Small (Traditional)

Here is a giant who is tall, tall, tall.
(Stand up tall.)
Here is an elf who is small, small, small.
(Squat.)
The elf who is small will try, try, try
(Slowly rise up.)
To reach the giant who is high, high, high.
(Stretch arms up high.)

Teddy Bear (Anonymous)

Teddy Bear, Teddy Bear,
Turn around.
Teddy Bear, Teddy Bear,
Touch the ground.

Teddy Bear, Teddy Bear,
Go upstairs.
Teddy Bear, Teddy Bear,
Say your prayers.

Teddy Bear, Teddy Bear,
Turn out the light.
Teddy Bear, Teddy Bear,
Spell goodnight.
G-O-O-D-N-I-G-H-T
Goodnight!

(Imitate designated movements.)

Ten Brave Firefighters (Adapted)

Ten brave firefighters sleeping in a row.
(Hold out hands, fingers parallel to floor.)
Ding goes the bell; down the pole they go.
(Imitate sliding down a pole with arms crossed
 at chest.)
Off in the engine, oh, oh, oh.
(Imitate driving engine.)
Using a big hose, so, so, so.
(Imitate holding hose.)
When all the fire is out, home they will go,
(Imitate driving truck.)
Back to their beds, all in a row.
(Hold out ten fingers.)

Ten Fat Turkeys (Adapted)

Ten fat turkeys standing in a row,
(Hold up ten fingers.)
They spread their wings and tails just so.
(Spread fingers wide.)
They strut to the left.
(Strut fingers left.)
They strut to the right.
(Strut fingers to right.)
They stand outside in the bright sunlight.
(Hold fingers up straight.)
Along comes a farmer with a great big gun.
(Pretend to look down barrel.)
Bang! Look at all those turkeys run!
(Clap hands loudly and flutter fingers away.)

Ten in the Bed (Traditional)

There were ten in the bed,
And the little one said,
"Roll over, roll over."
And they all rolled over,
And one fell out
There were nine in the bed,
And the little one said,
"Roll over, roll over."

(Continue until "then there were NONE in the
bed!")

Ten Little Indians (Traditional)

One little, two little, three little Indians,
Four little, five little, six little Indians,
Seven little, eight little, nine little Indians,
Ten little Indian boys.

(Repeat for girls.)

Ten Little Soldiers (Traditional)

Ten little soldiers standing in a row,
(Hold up ten fingers.)
They all bow down to the captain so.
(Bend fingers.)
They march to the left. They march to the right.
(March fingers left, then right.)
They stand up straight, ready to fight.
(Hold fingers straight up.)
Along comes a man with a great big gun.
(Imitate shooting gun.)
BANG! See those little soldiers run!
(Clap hands loudly, flutter fingers away.)

Ten Little Witches (Adapted)

(Tune: "Ten Little Indians")

One little, two little, three little witches,
Four little, five little, six little witches,
Seven little, eight little, nine little witches
Fly on Halloween night!

Ten Workers (Traditional)

Said the farmer, the miller, the baker,
"We'll give the dear baby his food."
Said the carpenter, glazier, and mason,
"We'll build him a house strong and good."
Said the weaver, the tailor, the cobbler,
"We'll make him warm pretty clothes."
The mechanic said, "I'll fix the auto
When off on a journey he goes."

Thanksgiving Friends (Adapted)

A little Indian climbed a tree to look and see
  what he could see.
(Imitate climbing tree and looking around.)
A little Pilgrim climbed one too and asked the
  Indian,
(Imitate climbing.)
"How do you do?"
(Extend hand as for handshake.)
The Indian raised his hand to send the Indian
  sign for a friend.
(Hold up index and middle fingers.)

There's Music in a Hammer
(Anonymous)

There's music in a hammer.
There's music in a nail.
There's music in a pussy cat
When you step on her tail.

There Was a Crooked Man
(Nursery Rhyme)

There was a crooked man,
And he walked a crooked mile.
He found a crooked sixpence
Upon a crooked stile.
He bought a crooked cat
Which caught a crooked mouse,
And they all lived together
In a crooked little house.

There Was an Old Woman
(Nursery Rhyme)

There was an old woman who lived in a shoe.
She had so many children she didn't know what
  to do.
She gave them some broth without any bread,
And whipped them all soundly and put them to
  bed.

This Is the Church (Traditional)

This is the church.
(Interlace fingers inside of hands.)
This is the steeple.
(Point and touch index fingers together.)
Open the door and see all the people.
(Turn hands palms out and wiggle fingers.)

This Is the Circle That Makes My Head
(Adapted)

This is the circle that makes my head.
(Arms overhead in circle.)
This is my mouth with which words are said.
(Point to mouth.)
These are my eyes with which I see.
(Point to eyes.)
This is my nose that's a part of me.
(Point to nose.)
This is the hair that grows on my head.
(Point to hair.)
This is my cap, all pretty and red.
(Make triangle on top of head with hands.)
Today I will finish my school for this year.
I'm one full year older. Everyone cheer!
(Clap hands and cheer.)

This Is What I Can Do (Traditional)

This is what I can do.
Everybody do it too.
This is what I can do.
Now I pass it on to you.

(Children stand in circle, singing, as one child
performs a movement for others to imitate. He or
she then points to another child to lead a new
action.)

This Little Calf (Traditional)

This little calf eats grass.
This little calf eats hay.
This little calf drinks water.
This little calf runs away.
This little calf does nothing,
But just lies down all day.

(Hold up five fingers; push down for each line.)

This Little Clown (Adapted)

This little clown is feeling sad.
This little clown is very mad.
This little clown is sleepy today.
This little clown is happy and gay.
This little clown so tiny and small,
He is afraid of everything tall.

(One finger for each line; imitate with facial expressions.)

This Little Pig (Nursery Rhyme)

This little pig went to market.
This little pig stayed home.
This little pig had roast beef.
This little pig had none.
And this little pig went
"Wee, wee, wee, wee" all the way home.

(Wiggle a finger for each line.)

This Old Man (Traditional)

This old man he played one.
He played knick-knack on my thumb.
With a knick-knack paddy-wack,
Give the dog a bone.
This old man came rolling home.
(Roll arms over and over.)

This old man he played two.
He played knick-knack on my shoe.
With a knick-knack paddy-wack,
Give the dog a bone.
This old man came rolling home.

This old man . . . three . . . knee.

This old man . . . four . . . floor.

This old man . . . five . . . hive.

This old man . . . six . . . sticks.

This old man . . . seven . . . heaven.

This old man . . . eight . . . gate.

This old man . . . nine . . . spine.

This old man . . . ten . . . once again.

The Three-cornered Hat (Traditional)

My hat it has three corners,
Three corners has my hat.
A hat without three corners
Could never be my hat.

Three Little Kittens (Nursery Rhyme)

Three little kittens, they lost their mittens,
And they began to cry:
"Oh, mother dear, see here, see here,
Our mittens we have lost."

"What, lost your mittens, you naughty kittens!
Then you shall have no pie.
Meow, meow, meow, meow,
Then you shall have no pie."

The three little kittens, they found their mittens,
And they began to cry:
"Oh mother dear, see here, see here,
Our mittens we have found!"

"What, found your mittens? You darling kittens.
Then you shall have some pie.
Meow, meow, meow, meow,
Then you shall have some pie."

Thumbkin Says, "I'll Dance" (Traditional)

Thumbkin says, "I'll dance."
Thumbkin says, "I'll dance."
Dancing, singing, merry little one,
Thumbkin says, "I'll dance again."

(Bounce thumbs up and down on table. Repeat, using Pointer, Tall Man, Ring Man, and Pinky.)

Tiger Walk (Traditional)

Walk, walk, softly—slow—
This is the way the tigers go.
Walk, walk, get out of the way,
Tigers are coming to school today!

(Imitate tiger walk.)

"To Bed! To Bed!" Says Sleepyhead (Nursery Rhyme)

"To bed! To bed!" says Sleepyhead.
"Tarry awhile," says Slow.
"Put on the pan," says Greedy Nan,
"We'll sup before we go."

To Market (Nursery Rhyme)

To market, to market to buy a fat pig.
Home again, home again, jiggety jig.
To market, to market to buy a fat hog.
Home again, home again, jiggety jog.

Tomorrow's the Fair (Anonymous)

Tomorrow's the fair,
And I shall be there,
Stuffing my guts
With gingerbread nuts.

Toot! Toot! (Anonymous)

A peanut sat on a railroad track;
His heart was all aflutter.
The five-fifteen came rushing by—
Toot! Toot! peanut butter!

To School (Cynthia Holley)

To school, to school,
I start my school today.
I'll work and nap,
And best, I'll get to play!

Touch My Hair (Traditional)

I touch my hair, my lips, my eyes.
I sit up straight; then I rise.
I touch my eyes, my nose, my chin,
And then I sit back down again.

(Imitate designated motions.)

Traffic Lights (Traditional)

"Stop," says the red light.
(Hold up hand.)
"Go," says the green.
(Point index finger.)
"Wait," says the yellow light,
(Open and shut hand.)
Blinking in between.
(Continue blinking.)

The Turkey (Traditional)

The turkey is a funny bird.
His head goes wobble, wobble.
All he says is just one word,
"Gobble, gobble, gobble!"

Twinkle, Twinkle, Little Star (Anonymous)

Twinkle, twinkle, little star,
(Open and close hands.)
How I wonder what you are!
(Open and close hands.)
Up above the world so high,
(Point to sky.)
Like a diamond in the sky.
(Make diamond with fingers.)
Twinkle, twinkle, little star,
(Open and close hands.)
How I wonder what you are!
(Open and close hands.)

Two Little Blackbirds (Nursery Rhyme)

Two little blackbirds sitting on a hill,
(Hold up each fist with thumbs pointed up.)
One named Jack, one named Jill.
(Wiggle one thumb, then the other.)
Fly away Jack, fly away Jill,
(Flutter each away behind back.)
Come back Jack, come back Jill.
(Fly thumbs back into position.)

Two Little Eyes (Traditional)

Two little eyes that open and close,
Two little ears and one little nose,
Two little cheeks and one little chin,
Two little lips with the teeth closed in!

(Point to designated parts.)

Two Little Hands Go Clap, Clap, Clap (Traditional)

Two little hands go clap, clap, clap.
Two little feet go tap, tap, tap.
One little body turns around
And sits quietly right down.

(Imitate designated movements.)

Two Little Hands So Clean and Bright (Traditional)

Two little hands so clean and bright,
(Hold up both hands.)
This is my left and this is my right.
(Wave left, then right hand.)

Two Little Houses (Traditional)

Two little houses all closed up tight,
(Hold up two fists.)
Open up the windows and let in the light.
(Open fists.)

Under the Spreading Chestnut Tree
(Traditional)

Under the spreading chestnut tree,
(Hands in circle overhead.)
When I held you on my knee,
(Slap knee.)
We were as happy as could be,
(Point to smiling face.)
Under the spreading chestnut tree.
(Hands in circle overhead.)

(Sing song replacing key words with motions.)

Unfortunately (Bobbi Katz)

Dinosaurs lived long ago.
They never had a chance to know
How many kids would love to get
A dinosaur to be their pet.

(Copyright 1976, by Bobbi Katz.)

Up a Step (Traditional)

Up a step, and up a step, and up a step, and
  up,
(Imitate climbing ladder.)
I climb the ladder to the very tiptop.
Then I slide down and zip to the ground!
(Slide one hand in swooping motion.)

Valentine's Good Morning (Adapted)

Good morning to you valentine.
How do you do?
Would you like to be my friend?
I made a heart for you!

Valentine (Cynthia Holley)

Here is a valentine.
I made it just for you
With paper and ribbons
And lots of Elmer's glue!
I cut it with my scissors
And designed it with my paint.
If I tell you that I love you,
Do you promise not to faint?

The Very Nicest Place (Anonymous)

The fish lives in the brook.
The bird lives in the tree.
But home's the very nicest place
For a little child like me.

Warm Hands (Traditional)

"Warm hands, warm!"
Do you know how?
If you want to warm your hands,
Rub them, rub them, now.

(Rub hands together.)

Way Down South (Anonymous)

Way down south where bananas grow,
A grasshopper stepped on an elephant's toe.
The elephant said, with tears in his eyes,
"Pick on somebody your own size."

Wee Willie Winkie (Anonymous)

Wee Willie Winkie runs through the town,
Upstairs, downstairs, in his nightgown.
Rapping at the windows, crying at the lock,
Are all the children in their beds?
For now it's eight o'clock!

We Wish You a Merry Christmas
(Traditional)

We wish you a merry Christmas.
We wish you a merry Christmas.
We wish you a merry Christmas
And a Happy New Year.

When Johnny Comes Marching Home
(Lambert)

When Johnny comes marching home again,
  hurrah! hurrah!
We'll give him a hearty welcome then, hurrah!
  hurrah!
The men will cheer, the boys will shout,
The ladies they will all turn out,
And we'll all feel great when Johnny comes
  marching home!

Where Is Thumbkin? *(Traditional)*

(Tune: "Are You Sleeping?")

Where is Thumbkin? Where is Thumbkin?
Here I am, here I am.
(Hold up each thumb.)
How are you today sir?
(Wiggle thumbs.)
Very well, I thank you!
Run away, run away!
(Run thumbs behind back.)

(Repeat with other fingers.)
Where is Pointer . . .

Where is Tall Man . . .

Where is Ringer . . .

Where is Pinky . . .

Whisky, Frisky *(Traditional)*

Whisky, frisky, hippity hop,
Up he goes to the treetop,
(Hold up one arm and crawl other hand up.)
Whirly, twirly, 'round and 'round,
Down he scampers to the ground.
(Crawl hand down extended arm.)
Furly, curly, what a tail,
(Wave arm like a tail.)
Tall as a feather, broad as a sail.
(Hold hands up high, then wide apart.)
Where's his supper? In the shell.
(Hold hands together in ball.)
Snappy, cracky, out it fell.
(Let hands fall apart.)

White Coral Bells *(Nursery Rhyme)*

White coral bells upon a slender stalk,
Lilies of the valley deck my garden walk.
Oh, don't you wish that you could hear them
  ring?
That only happens when the fairies sing.

Who Feels Happy? *(Traditional)*

Who feels happy? Who feels gay?
All who do clap their hands this way. *(clap,
  clap)*
Who feels happy? Who feels gay?
All who do nod their heads this way. *(nod, nod)*

(Repeat with the following body parts.)
. . . stamp your feet . . .

. . . wave your hands . . .

. . . tap your shoulders . . .

Wiggle *(Adapted)*

Wiggle fingers,
Wiggle toes,
Wiggle shoulders,
Wiggle nose.
No more wiggles are left in me,
So I sit in my chair as still as can be.

(Imitate designated movements.)

Will You Be My Valentine? *(Adapted)*

Will you be my valentine, valentine, valentine?
Will you be my valentine? I love you!

Yes, I'll be your valentine, valentine, valentine.
Yes, I'll be your valentine. I love you!

The Wind *(Anonymous)*

I come to work as well as play.
I'll tell you what I do.
I whistle all the livelong day,
"Woo-oo-oo-oo! Woo-oo!"
I toss the branches up and down
And shake them to and fro.
I whirl the leaves in flocks of brown
And send them high and low.
I strew the twigs upon the ground.
The frozen earth I sweep;
I blow the children 'round and 'round
And wake the flowers from sleep.

The Witch's Haunted House (Adapted)*

(TUNE: "FARMER IN THE DELL")

The witch's haunted house, the witch's haunted
   house.
Beware, it's Halloween at the witch's haunted
   house.

The witch takes a cat, the witch takes a cat.
Beware, it's Halloween at the witch's haunted
   house.

The cat takes the bat . . .

The bat takes the ghost . . .

The ghost says, "Boo!"

Woodchuck (Traditional)

How much wood would a woodchuck chuck,
If a woodchuck could chuck wood?

(Repeat over and over, faster each time.)

Yankee Doodle (Traditional)

Yankee Doodle came to town riding on a pony.
Stuck a feather in his hat and called it macaroni.
Yankee Doodle keep it up.
Yankee Doodle Dandy.
Mind the music and the step,
And with the girls be handy.

A Young Lady of Lynn (Anonymous)

There was a young lady of Lynn,
Who was so uncommonly thin
That when she essayed
To drink lemonade,
She slipped through the straw and fell in.

The Zoo (Cynthia Holley)

Oh, it's such fun to go to the zoo.
We'll see lions, bears, and a kangaroo.
Be careful near the monkey cage;
Those little guys can make such a rage.
And don't go swimming with a seal;
He might make you his lunchtime meal!

Recipes for Crafts and Creations

Bubble Solution

3 C. water
1 C. liquid soap
1 Tb. sugar

Mix ingredients well. Use solution in science experiments and related activities.

Candles

Commercial candle wax (paraffin)
Wick
Colored crayons or candle dye
Small stick
Can of water

Heat wax in top of a double boiler. Tie wick to the stick. Carefully supervise children as they take turns, one at a time, dipping the wick into the wax. To build up a candle, they must dip, wait several seconds, and dip again. When the candle is formed, dip into can of cold water to set.

Clay #1

4 C. all-purpose flour
1 1/2 C. water
1 C. salt
A few drops of food coloring (optional)

Mix all ingredients in bowl. Knead 10 minutes. Roll dough 1/4" thick and cut with cookie cutters of various shapes, or mold into shapes. Poke hole with pencil in top of shapes. Bake at 250 degrees F for 2 hours, or until hard. Cool, paint, varnish, string with yarn, and hang.

Clay #2

1 C. salt
1/2 C. cornstarch
1/2 C. boiling water
A few drops of food coloring (optional)

Heat ingredients, stirring constantly until mixture is too thick to stir. Cool and knead until smooth into desired shapes. Dry and paint as desired.

Collage Paste

1 C. all-purpose flour
1 C. water
2 C. boiling water
1 tsp. alum
1 tsp. oil of wintergreen

Mix flour into 1 C. of water. Then slowly add 2 C. of boiling water. Cook in double boiler over low heat until smooth. Add alum and oil of wintergreen and cook the mixture. Store in closed container in cool place.

Face Paint

2 tsp. Crisco
2 1/2 tsp. cornstarch
1 tsp. white flour
3–4 drops glycerin
Food coloring
Cold cream

Mix first three ingredients with rubber spatula to form a smooth paste. Add 3–4 drops glycerin for a creamy consistency. Add food coloring as desired.

Apply thin layer of cold cream to child's face. Apply face paint (it's nontoxic if swallowed) in a thin coat over cold cream, avoiding eyes. Recipe paints one child.

Fingerpaint #1

2 Tb. sugar
2 C. cold water
1/2 C. cornstarch
Food coloring

Mix sugar and cornstarch. Slowly add water and cook over low heat, stirring constantly until blended. Divide into portions and add desired food colorings. Clean up with soapy water.

Fingerpaint #2

3 C. water
1 C. commercial wallpaper paste powder
Food coloring
1 C. salt (optional)

Stir powder into water. Divide into portions and add food colorings as desired. You may add 1 C. of salt to the mixture for a different tactile sensation.

Glowing Garden

2 or 3 porous rocks
5 or 6 pieces charcoal
1/4 C. ammonia
1/4 C. salt
1/4 C. liquid bluing
1/4 C. water
Food coloring, if desired

Put charcoal and rocks in shallow bowl. Combine other ingredients and pour over charcoal. Beautiful, colorful crystals will form immediately.

Papier Mâché

1 C. wheat paste
10 C. water
Newspaper

Mix wheat paste and water until smooth. Soak newspaper strips in mixture and wrap several layers around a balloon or other items. Dry well. Paint with tempera paints and decorate as desired.

Playdough #1

3 C. all-purpose flour
2 C. salt
3 Tb. cooking oil
2 to 3 C. water
A few drops of food coloring (optional)

Mix ingredients and store in container, preferably in refrigerator.

Playdough #2

2 C. flour
1/2 C. salt
1 Tb. alum
1 1/2 C. water
1 Tb. cooking oil
A few drops of food coloring (optional)

Bring water to boil. Add cooking oil and food coloring. Add dry ingredients. Mix and knead until smooth. Store in plastic bag or container, preferably in refrigerator.

Soap Suds Snow

4 C. mild soap flakes
1/2 C. water

Slowly add water to flakes in a bowl and whip until dough is of a consistency that can be rolled into snowballs or formed into other shapes. Tint pink with food coloring to make "cotton candy."

Snow Paint

1 C. mild soap flakes
1 C. water
Food coloring

Whip soap flakes into water with a mixer until thick and stiff. Divide and put into small cups and add food coloring, if desired. Paint "snow" onto paper to make gingerbread people, flowers, rainbows, or other objects.

Recipes for Snacks and Meals

The following recipes have been selected because they can be used to promote awareness of good eating practices. Because it is important to develop good eating habits at a young age, nutrition should be an integral part of every early childhood program. The early childhood classroom is an ideal place to introduce new and healthy foods to young children.

All the recipes here have been reviewed by a licensed nutritionist and given approval as appropriate for young children. Though during holiday times the early childhood program may offer cookies or other special treats, the authors strongly encourage preschool programs to offer only nutritious snacks.

Ants on a Log

1 bunch celery
1 C. peanut butter
1 small package raisins

Clean celery stalks, remove leaves, and cut stalks into two pieces. Fill celery with peanut butter. Place raisins on top to look like ants walking along a log. Serves 15–18 children.

Apple Crisp

1 dozen apples
1 C. brown sugar
1/2 C. granulated sugar
1 C. whole-wheat flour
1 Tb. cinnamon
1 tsp. nutmeg
2/3 C. butter or margarine

Peel and slice apples; put into greased 9" x 12" pan. Blend remaining ingredients until crumbly and spread over apples. Bake at 375 degrees F for about 30 minutes. If top browns before apples are baked, cover with foil for the last few minutes. Serves 12–15 children.

Apple Sailboats

6 cheese slices, cut in half to make 12 triangles
12 apple slices
12 toothpicks

Weave toothpick through cheese slice. Poke toothpick into apple slice to make sailboat.

Astronaut Roll-ups

4 McIntosh apples
4 navel oranges
2 Tb. butter

Peel, core, and slice apples. Peel and seed oranges. Purée fruit in blender or food processor. Lightly butter 15" x 10" x 1" pan. Using a rubber spatula, spread the fruit into the pan. Bake at 200 degrees F for 3 hours, with the door slightly ajar. Remove when dry, cut into 12 pieces. Place pieces on waxed paper and roll them up!

Baby's Applesauce

12 apples
3 Tb. sugar (optional)
3 C. water
Cinnamon

Peel, core, and slice apples. Put in saucepan with water and cook until mushy. Add sugar and sprinkle with a bit of cinnamon. Serves 24 children.

Baked Apples

12 apples
3/4 C. brown sugar
2 to 3 C. water
Cinnamon, if desired

Cut core from apples and put brown sugar inside. Sprinkle with cinnamon and place in large baking pan, adding enough water to cover bottom of pan. Bake at 400 degrees F for 30–45 minutes, basting frequently.

Banana Coconut Snowmen

1/2 banana per child
1 Tb. honey per child
1/2 C. milk per child
1/3 C. shredded coconut per child
Toothpicks
Raisins
Carrot, cut in tiny pieces

Give each child one large, one medium, and one small piece of banana. Stir honey into milk. Dip pieces into milk and roll in coconut. Stack pieces and secure with toothpick. Decorate with toothpick arms, carrot nose, raisin eyes, and buttons.

Bendable Biscuits

2 C. all-purpose flour
3 Tb. baking powder
1/2 tsp. salt
1/2 C. shortening
3/4 C. milk

Combine flour, baking powder, and salt. Using pastry blender or fork, cut in shortening until coarse balls form. Add milk and stir to form dough. Turn dough onto floured surface and sprinkle lightly with flour. Knead until no longer sticky, adding flour as needed. Roll to 1/2" thickness and cut with floured cookie cutters or roll into desired shapes. Place 1/2" apart on un-greased cookie sheet and bake at 450 degrees F for 10–12 minutes, or until golden brown. Makes a dozen biscuits.

Butter

2 C. heavy cream
Small jars with lids

Pour small amount of very cold cream into jars. Children shake jars until cream forms a smooth paste.

Celery Boats

1 lb. carton low-fat cottage cheese
1 C. crushed pineapple (packed in natural juice), drained
1 bunch of celery

Wash celery stalks well and cut into 3"–4" pieces. Mix pineapple and cottage cheese together and spread onto celery. Serves 20–24 children.

Cereal Balls

1/2 C. ground shredded wheat cereal
1 tsp. honey
1 Tb. peanut butter
1 Tb. milk
2 Tb. wheat germ

Measure the above ingredients into a cup and stir with a spoon. Shape into balls with hands and roll in wheat germ. Serves 1 child.

Cereal Snack Sacks

1 large box Corn Chex
1 large box Cheerios
1 large box Mini-wheats
1 large box Puffed Rice

Count out and put in a plastic sack 10 pieces of each of the above cereals. Shake the bag to mix them up. Serves 24–30 children.

Christmas Cookies

1 C. sugar
1 C. soft butter or margarine
3 Tb. cream or milk
1 tsp. vanilla
1 egg
3 C. all-purpose flour
1 1/2 tsp. baking powder
1/2 tsp. salt

In large bowl, combine first 5 ingredients; blend well. Stir in remaining ingredients; blend well. Chill dough for easier handling. Heat oven to 400 degrees F. Roll dough 1/3 at a time on floured surface to 1/8" thickness. Cut with floured cookie cutter. Place 1" apart on ungreased cookie sheet. If desired, sprinkle with colored sugar or paint with Egg Yolk Cookie Paint (see recipe on p. 111). Bake at 400 degrees F for 5–8 minutes, or until edges are light brown (don't overbake). Immediately remove from cookie sheet. Makes 5–6 dozen cookies.

Circus Popcorn

1 Tb. oil
1/2 C. popcorn
Salt (optional)

In popcorn popper or heavy pan, pour oil and place two kernels of corn. Cook over medium heat. When the sample kernels pop, add the rest of the corn. Cover and continue popping until most of the kernels have popped. (On a stove it may be necessary to shake the pan occasionally to avoid burning the corn.) Pour into small paper bags, top with a little salt if desired, and serve.

Corn on the Cob

1 dozen ears corn
1 very big pot unsalted water
1 bottle squeeze margarine
Salt and pepper

Quality corn on the cob has green husks that are not dried or decayed on the ends. To test for juiciness, poke a kernel to see if it squirts. Shuck, and throw away the husks and silks of the corn. Wash ears of corn well. Carefully put corn in large pan of boiling water. Cover and boil for 5–8 minutes, until tender. Serve with butter, salt, and pepper as desired.

Curds and Whey

1 quart light cream
2 Tb. buttermilk
1 tsp. salt

Pour cream into large pan and cook over medium heat until warm (not hot). Stir in buttermilk, cover pan, and remove from stove. Store in a place with a moderate temperature (not in refrigerator and not too warm). In 1–2 days it should look thick, similar to yogurt. Cover a colander with 2 layers of cheesecloth and pour thickened cream into it. The thick part in the colander is the curds, and the liquid that pours through is the whey. Place another cheesecloth on top of the curds and wrap the colander in foil or plastic wrap. Continue to drain the colander overnight. The next day put the curds into a bowl and mix in salt. Store in refrigerator. Spread on crackers or bread to eat.

Dinosaur's Salad

1 head iceberg lettuce
1 bunch fresh spinach
1 head leaf lettuce
1 bunch celery
1 zucchini squash
1 green pepper
1 green onion
1 cucumber
Any other "edible plants"

Clean vegetables well. Cut into pieces and toss together in a large bowl. Serve in individual bowls, offering a variety of salad dressings. Makes 12 snack salads.

Edible Peanut Butter Playdough

4 Tb. peanut butter
4 Tb. honey
Powdered milk

Mix ingredients with hands, adding powdered milk little by little until mixture forms a dough with body that does not stick to fingers. Shape into desired forms, or roll out and cut with cookie cutters. Serves 2–3 children.

Eggnog

4 eggs
1/3 C. honey
4 C. cold milk
1 tsp. vanilla
Pinch of nutmeg

Beat eggs with honey. Add milk and vanilla and beat until frothy. Pour into cups and sprinkle with nutmeg. Makes about 10 servings.

Egg Yolk Cookie Paint

3 egg yolks
1 tsp. water
1 tsp. sugar
Food coloring

Beat first 3 ingredients with mixer. Put in little cups and add food color to each cup. Paint cookies and bake.

Fingerfood Friends

Apple slices
Pear halves
Carrot sticks
Popcorn
Cereal
Bread sticks
Olives
Grapes
Lettuce leaves
Raisins
Nuts
Red pepper strips

Put large assortment of foods on a tray. Children use a pear half for the body of a "fingerfood friend." They can make a lettuce skirt, olive feet, cereal hair, raisin eyes, bread stick arms— whatever they like—to create an edible person.

Fingerpaint Pudding

2 packages instant pudding mix (preferably
sugar free)
Milk

Prepare pudding mix as directed on package.
Children paint with the pudding as they would
with ordinary fingerpaint. But with this special
fingerpaint, they can lick their fingers to "clean
up." One package will make enough paint for 8
children.

Fourth of July Fruit Cup

1 quart strawberries
1 quart blueberries
1 bunch bananas

Clean berries, remove stems, and place berries
in a large bowl. Peel and slice bananas into the
bowl. Toss lightly. Serve this red, white, and blue
snack in cups or small bowls. Serves 24 children.

French Toast

2 eggs
1 C. milk
6 slices of bread
6 pats of butter

Beat eggs and milk in large pan. Dip slices of
bread into mixture and fry with a bit of butter.
Serve with syrup, powdered sugar, or jelly.
Makes 6 pieces of toast.

Fresh Fruit Salad

2 apples
2 oranges
1 pineapple
2 pears
2 peaches
Other fruits in season
2 C. plain or vanilla yogurt
2 Tb. honey

Cut various fruits into bite-size pieces and mix
together in large bowl. Mix honey into yogurt and
pour over fruit salad. Serves 12–15 children.

Garden Salad

Head of lettuce
2 carrots
2 stalks of celery
1 cucumber
2 tomatoes
1 zucchini
4 mushrooms
Sprouts

Wash and drain all vegetables well. Peel and cut
into pieces. Combine in large bowl and toss.
Serve with various kinds of dressings. Makes
8–10 servings.

Garlic Bread

2 loaves Italian bread
1 lb. butter or margarine
Garlic powder

Slice bread and spread with softened butter.
Sprinkle a little garlic powder on each slice. Bake
at 400 degrees F until toasted. Serves 24 children.

Gelatin Cubes

4 envelopes unflavored gelatin
3 packages flavored gelatin
4 C. boiling water

Put all packages of gelatin into a large bowl.
Slowly add water and stir until dissolved. Pour
into 9" x 13" baking pan and chill until firm. Cut
into squares, or use cookie cutter shapes.
Serves 15–20 children.

Hot Chocolate

1 C. *very warm* milk per child
1–2 Tb. hot chocolate mix per child
Miniature marshmallows

Let each child stir chocolate mix into cup of milk
and then count out 5–6 marshmallows to top
drink.

Humpty Dumpty Eggs

1 dozen eggs
1/4 C. milk
2 Tb. butter

Children break eggs, letting "Humpty Dumpty" (without the shell) fall into large bowl. Add milk. With wire whisk, beat eggs. Melt butter in skillet and add eggs. Stir until eggs begin to harden. Scrambled eggs are ready when slightly moist but set. Serves 12–15 children.

Individual Pizzas

2 packages English muffins
24 oz. can tomato sauce
Oregano, garlic, and spices
Beef and sausage pieces
Onion, mushroom, etc. pieces
24 slices of mozzarella cheese

Split muffins and spread with tomato sauce. Sprinkle small amount of desired spices. Top with meat and vegetables as desired. Place cheese slice on top. Bake at 450 degrees F for about 20 minutes. Makes 24 pizzas.

Latkes

2 large potatoes
1/4 C. all-purpose flour
1 egg
1/2 tsp. salt

Peel and grate potatoes. Mix remaining ingredients and add to potatoes. Pour tiny pancakes onto hot griddle or skillet. Fry until brown on both sides. Makes about 1 dozen.

Lentil Soup

1 C. dry lentils
3 C. water
1/4 C. brown sugar
1 tsp. salt
2 slices bacon, cut into pieces
1 small onion
1 C. water
1/4 C. catsup
1/4 C. molasses

Wash lentils well. Heat in water to boiling; simmer covered for 20–30 minutes, or until tender. Drain and stir in remaining ingredients, simmering for another 20 minutes, stirring occasionally. Add more water as needed. Serves 10–12 children.

Miss Cindy's Favorite Gingerbread People

1 C. soft butter or margarine
1/2 C. brown sugar
1/2 C. granulated sugar
1 C. molasses
1/2 C. milk
5 C. flour
1 tsp. salt
1 tsp. baking soda
1 Tb. ginger
1/2 tsp. nutmeg

Combine first five ingredients in large bowl, blending well. Sift dry ingredients together and stir into mixture. Chill dough 3 hours or overnight. Divide dough into 2 balls and roll on floured surface to 1/8" thickness. Cut with floured cookie cutters and decorate with raisins, red cinnamon drops, or dried fruit pieces. With spatula carefully place on lightly greased cookie sheets and bake at 375 degrees F for 7–12 minutes. Remove immediately and cool on wire rack. Makes about 3 dozen gingerbread people.

Miss Faraday's Stone Soup

1 large, *clean* stone
4 C. water
3 carrots, peeled and chopped
4 potatoes, peeled and cut
1 onion, cut into tiny pieces
1 large can stewed tomatoes
1 can corn
1 can peas
1 tsp. salt
1/2 tsp. pepper
3 bouillon cubes

Put water and stone in large pot. Add fresh vegetables, which the children have helped prepare, and boil until nearly soft. Add tomatoes, corn, peas, bouillon, salt, and pepper. Cook 15–20 minutes longer. Remove the stone and serve.

Monkey Sandwiches

Large bag of peanuts
1 tsp. oil
6 bananas

Shell peanuts and remove skins. Put peanuts and oil into peanut-butter machine or blender. Blend until smooth. Split bananas and spread peanut butter on them. Serves 12 children.

No-Bake Yummies

1 C. granola cereal
1 small package peanut butter chips
1 C. honey
1 C. shredded coconut
1 C. raisins
1 C. sesame seeds
1 C. light corn syrup

Mix ingredients and roll into small balls. Chill and eat. Serves 10–12 children.

Old-fashioned Lemonade

8 lemons
1 3/4 C. sugar
2 quarts water
2 C. ice cubes

Cut and squeeze juice from lemons. Add to water in large pitcher. Stir in sugar and ice cubes. Garnish with lemon slices. Makes 2 1/2 quarts.

Parlor Pack Ice Cream

3 eggs
2 C. sugar
2 quarts milk
2 pints cream
2 Tb. vanilla
Dash of salt
Fruit pieces, if desired
8 lb. crushed ice
1 1/4 lb. rock salt

Blend eggs and sugar well. Add milk, cream, vanilla, and salt, stirring constantly. Pour into freezer can. Crank, alternately adding crushed ice and rock salt. When handle becomes difficult to turn, ice cream is thick. Add fruit if desired and crank a few more times.

Perfect Peanut Butter Cookies

1 C. granulated sugar
1 C. brown sugar
1 C. butter or margarine
1 C. peanut butter
1/4 C. milk
1 Tb. vanilla
2 eggs
3 C. flour
2 tsp. soda
1 tsp. salt

Mix first 7 ingredients with mixer. Blend in remaining ingredients, stirring well. Shape into 1" balls and place 2" apart on ungreased cookie sheet. Flatten crisscross style with fork dipped in flour, or mold into desired shapes. Bake in 375 degrees F oven for 10–12 minutes. Makes about 3 dozen cookies.

Personalized Pretzels

1 pkg. dry yeast
1/2 C. warm water
1 egg
1/4 C. honey
1 tsp. salt
1/4 C. margarine
1 C. low-fat milk
5 C. all-purpose flour
Coarse salt

Sprinkle and dissolve yeast into warm water. Mix egg yolk, margarine, and milk into the yeast. Add salt and enough flour to make thick, easy-to-handle dough. Knead dough on floured surface for 5 minutes. Let rise 1 hour. Divide into 20 pieces. Roll the dough into "snakes" and form into desired shapes. Place on cookie sheet and brush with beaten egg white. Sprinkle with coarse salt as desired. Bake at 425 degrees F about 17 minutes, until golden brown. Makes 20 pretzels.

Pooh's Pancakes

2 C. flour
1/2 tsp. salt
3 tsp. baking powder
1/4 C. wheat germ
2 Tb. honey
2 eggs
1 1/2 C. low-fat milk
1/4 C. oil

In large mixing bowl, beat eggs. Stir in oil, honey, and milk. Add remaining ingredients, stirring until most of the lumps are gone. Pour batter 1/4 cup at a time onto hot griddle or skillet. When bubbles appear on the surface, flip and bake on other side. One medium and two small round pancakes make a cute bear face!

Serve with honey, or set out a variety of toppings (fresh fruit, powdered sugar, maple syrup, cinnamon) for the children to try. Makes about 2 dozen medium-size pancakes.

Popsicles

1 quart yogurt
1 quart fruit juice

Blend juice and yogurt and pour into ice cube trays or muffin tins. Place wooden spoon or stick into each section. Freeze. Makes 24 small popsicles.

Pudding Tarts

2 packages instant pudding mix (preferably sugar free)
Milk
1 dozen ready-made tart shells, baked
1 pint heavy cream
4 Tb. sugar
1 tsp. vanilla

Prepare pudding mix according to package directions. Pour into individual shells. With a chilled bowl and beaters, beat cream until slightly thickened. Add sugar and vanilla and whip until thick. Do not overbeat. Spoon on top of tarts and serve. Serves 12 children.

Pumpkin Pie

2 eggs
3/4 C. sugar
1 tsp. cinnamon
1/2 tsp. salt
1/2 tsp. ginger
1/2 tsp. nutmeg
2 C. canned or cooked pumpkin
1 can evaporated milk (13 oz.)
Ready-made pie shell

Beat eggs slightly, and add remaining ingredients, blending well. Pour mixture into pie shell and bake at 425 degrees F for 15 minutes. Reduce temperature to 350 degrees F and bake about 45 minutes more, or until knife inserted into middle comes out clean.

Pumpkin Seeds

2 C. pumpkin seeds
2 Tb. oil
1 tsp. salt (optional)

Wash seeds well and stir with oil in bowl. Spread out on cookie sheet and sprinkle salt on top. Bake at 250 degrees F until crisp and slightly brown.

Quickest Bread

1/4 C. wheat germ
1 C. molasses
2 C. buttermilk
2 tsp. soda
1/4 tsp. salt
4 C. whole wheat flour

Mix wheat germ, molasses, and buttermilk. Stir in soda and salt. Add flour one cup at a time, blending well. Bake in large greased loaf pan at 375 degrees F for 30–40 minutes. Slice and serve with honey or butter. Makes one loaf.

Rainbow Toast

1 loaf square white sandwich bread
1 pint milk
Food coloring

Pour milk into several cups and tint with food coloring. Cut a slice of bread to make two triangles and place one triangle on top of a square piece of bread to resemble a house with a roof. Using *clean* paint brushes (or Q-tips), paint the houses with the milk solution. Place on cookie sheet and toast lightly in oven. Serve with cream cheese or butter for snack. One loaf serves 10–12 children.

Shape Kabobs

1 pineapple
1 lb. cheese, such as monterey jack or cheddar (not sliced)
1 small canned ham

Clean and cut pineapple into cubes. Cut cheese into balls (with melon baller) and cut ham into triangles. Arrange on a toothpick. Serves 24–30 children.

S'Mores

1 package of graham crackers
1 dozen milk chocolate candy bars
1 bag of large marshmallows

Put 1/2 candy bar (4 squares) onto 1/2 graham cracker. Toast 2 marshmallows on a stick. Put hot marshmallow on top of chocolate and top with other half of graham cracker. Serves 24 children.

Snow Cones

Crushed ice
Frozen concentrated juice (fruit punch or orange)

Put crushed ice in paper cups. Pour 2–3 tablespoons of liquid concentrate over ice.

Spaghetti and Meatballs

1 lb. ground beef
1/2 C. bread crumbs
1/2 small onion, finely chopped
1/4 C. grated parmesan cheese
1/4 tsp. salt
Pinch of pepper
1/4 C. wheat germ
1 egg
1 Tb. oil
Large jar of spaghetti sauce
2 packages spaghetti noodles (32 oz. total)

In large bowl, combine first 9 ingredients. Mix well with spoon, then shape into 2" balls. Fry in large skillet with oil. Drain and add jar of spaghetti sauce. Cook spaghetti noodles according to directions on package. Serve meatballs and sauce over hot noodles. Sprinkle a little more cheese on top. Makes 12–15 small servings.

Sprouting Sprouts

2 Tb. alfalfa seeds
1 quart glass jar
Cheesecloth and rubber band

Place seeds in jar and fill about half full of water. Soak overnight. The next day cover with cheesecloth secured with rubber band. Pour off water. Each day rinse seeds with fresh water and drain well. Put jar into paper towel or sack to keep out the light. On the fourth day expose the sprouts to light and they will turn green. Cut them and add to your salad. Store in refrigerator.

Strawberry Milkshakes

2 C. strawberries
6 C. milk
2 C. small ice cubes
2 Tb. sugar

Blend all ingredients in blender. Pour into cups and drink with a straw. Serves 12–15 children.

Trail Mix

1 small box raisins
1 small jar peanuts
1 small jar sesame sticks
1 small bag pretzels

Mix all ingredients together and divide into individual sacks or cups.

Witch's Brew

2 quarts apple cider or juice
2 Tb. cloves
4 cinnamon sticks
1 orange
1 sliced lemon

Pierce orange with fork and stick cloves into it. Put all ingredients into saucepan and warm over low heat. Strain and serve.

Yogurt Drink

1 quart vanilla yogurt
1 quart milk
1 quart fresh or frozen fruit

Combine all ingredients in a large bowl. Blend on medium speed with an electric mixer. Pour into cups and drink with a straw. Serves 12 children.

Reproducible Resources

The worksheets and patterns here are organized seasonally and thematically in the typical sequence they are presented in a preschool or kindergarten classroom—the sequence that is used in *Every Day in Every Way: A Year-Round Calendar of Preschool Learning Challenges.*

They should follow discussions about and hands-on experience with the concepts they deal with. Use worksheets and patterns flexibly, depending on the developmental level of your students. Because each classroom contains children of varying ages and abilities, the teacher should offer activities that will challenge the children but not make them feel pressured to perform a task at which they will not be able to succeed. For example, most 5-year-olds demonstrate an interest in cutting with scissors, but not all 5-year-olds will be capable of cutting out a circle. And 3-year-olds who are capable of cutting successfully should not be denied the opportunity to use a scissors.

The following worksheets and patterns are designed to span the ability levels of the children in a typical early childhood program. Although not every child in every program will be able to experience success with each activity, it has been found that most children derive great enjoyment from these activities. If you encounter a child who does not exhibit the maturity for a particular task, you might consider the following approaches:

1. Assist the child with the task. You could, for example, hold and turn the paper as the child cuts.
2. Adapt the activity. The child could be asked to write the first letter of his or her name rather than the full name.
3. Offer an alternate activity. If a child does not want to cut out items for a calendar, he or she may be willing to remove pictures from the old calendar on the bulletin board.

Teacher's Guide for Reproducible Resources

The Schoolbus, page 131

This worksheet may accompany a discussion about transportation, beginning school, safety rules, or shapes. Help the children cut out the wheels and paste them on the bus. The children can color the bus. They or the teacher can write their names on the worksheet.

My Mirror, page 132

Use this worksheet with activities and discussions relating to body parts and self-concept. Help the children print their names on the worksheet. They draw and color their face in the mirror.

What's Missing, pages 133 and 134

Use these worksheets with activities and discussions naming body parts and their functions. Have the students complete the pictures by putting in the missing parts and coloring the pictures.

On, Under, Next To, and In Front Of, page 135

Spatial relation concepts can be introduced and reinforced with these pictures, which can be used in a variety of ways. A felt strip can be glued on the back of each one, and the children can place them on a flannelboard according to the teacher's directions. Or you can place the items on the flannelboard and ask the students to identify where they are located in relation to one another.

These pictures can also be duplicated for the children to color and cut out. Direct them to paste the patterns on a sheet of paper following directions such as "Paste the house near the bottom of the page; paste the tree next to the house; paste the dog under the tree; paste the car in front of the garage; paste the apples on the tree." Encourage the children to tell a story about their completed picture.

Fingerpuppets with Feelings, page 136

This activity is useful with a discussion about feelings and emotions. Help the children color and cut out the puppets and tape them together to fit each child's fingers. Children can improve their manual dexterity by holding up specific fingers in answer to questions such as, How would you feel if a big bear started to chase you? What kind of face would you wear if it rained and you could not go to the park for a picnic? How would you look if you received a new bicycle for your birthday?

Weather Chart, page 137

This chart can be used in daily discussions of the weather as well as in discussions of seasons. Write a new date each week on the calendar and hang it in a location convenient for group use.

Weather Pictures, page 138
More Weather Pictures, page 139

These pictures accompany the Weather Chart. Color or highlight with markers, cut out, and sort into envelopes for the children to select and place on the chart each day.

During a unit on weather, the children can be given individual Weather Charts and helped to color, cut out, and paste the weather pictures on their charts.

Fall Favorites, page 140

This worksheet reinforces the concept of "same and different" and develops visual discrimination and fine motor skills. As a follow-up to activities in which children visually discriminate concrete objects as the same and different, they can locate and color the items in each row on this worksheet that are the same.

Hidden Halloween Ghosts, page 141

Visual discrimination and figure-ground perception skills are reinforced in this worksheet. Children search for ghosts that are hidden in this picture and circle them and then color the picture. Help the students count the number of hidden ghosts that they found. Encourage them to tell a story about the picture.

Shape-a-Picture, page 142

This pattern can be duplicated on construction paper or standard bond paper, and the shapes can be cut out by the teacher or the students. They can be arranged to form any number of objects and pasted in place. Crayons or markers can be used to add details, such as facial features or tails. A felt strip can be glued to the back of each shape for use on a flannelboard. These shapes can also be covered with clear adhesive plastic and used by the children in sorting, matching, and classifying activities.

Halloween Patterns, page 143
More Halloween Patterns, page 144

These pictures can be used in a variety of ways during the Halloween season. The teacher can decorate them with markers or crayons and cut them out. A felt strip can be glued on the back of each one for use on a flannelboard; the pumpkin, witch, jack-o-lantern, and ghost can be duplicated and used on the flannelboard with Halloween fingerplays. These pictures can also be used to decorate the classroom bulletin board or windows, or they can be hung as a mobile.

Children can sort them by color or place them in patterns, copying examples laid out by the teacher. They can be hidden in the classroom for the children to find and identify. The children can be asked to describe the pictures that they found and see if classmates can identify them from the clues they give. Or you can give clues that will enrich vocabulary; for example, "I'm looking for something that is black. It flies in the sky. It has an ugly face and wears a pointed hat. It is mean and wicked. Who can find this picture?" Patterns can also be duplicated and used to reinforce math skills such as counting and identifying sets with the most or fewest objects.

Bat Pattern, page 145

Children develop skills of eye-hand coordination with this holiday art project. This pattern is reproduced onto black paper and used with two egg carton sections to make a bat. Help children cut out and decorate the bat as indicated in the directions. Bats can be hung with rubber bands from the ceiling.

Brother to Sister Maze, #1, page 146
Sister to Brother Maze, #2, page 147

Eye-hand coordination and left-to-right progression are developed with this pre-writing activity. Children should be encouraged to follow the path with their finger before they complete these worksheets with a pencil or crayon. Use one or both worksheets, depending on the maturity of your students. For younger students, apply a line of glue on the path and have them be "Hansel" and sprinkle crumbs or croutons along the path from the brother to the sister.

Family Members, page 148

These figures can be utilized to teach many concepts. They can be colored, cut out, covered with clear adhesive plastic, and made to stand up with tabs or used on the flannelboard. They can be attached to tongue depressors and used as puppets. Each puppet can "speak" in the respective family member's voice. Children enjoy dramatizing with family figures as well as following directions such as, Place the younger brother beside the mother, and the older sister beside the father, or Line up the family from smallest to largest. Figures can also be duplicated to form sets. Have the children copy and extend patterns laid out by the teacher. Family members can also be used with the house pattern on page 149.

House Pattern, page 149

This pattern can be used with the Family Members, page 148, in flannelboard and dramatization activities.

Certificates, page 150

Use these certificates when discussing families and where they live, or safety rules. Songs, games, and discussions at home as well as in school can be used to teach young children their address and phone number. When a child can state his or her address and phone number, award a certificate. Fill in the child's name, address, and phone number. Have the child color the certificate with bright colored markers. Pin or string with yarn for the child to wear home. The certificates can also be hung on the wall or from the ceiling.

Complete the Houses, page 151

This worksheet may accompany activities and discussions about houses. Skills of visual closure, eye-hand coordination, and discrimination are developed as children complete this worksheet. Identification and reproduction of basic shapes are also reinforced with this activity.

Dot-to-Dot Teepee, page 152

Use this worksheet when studying Thanksgiving, Indians, or types of houses. Help children locate and connect dots to complete the picture. The finished picture can be colored. Ask questions such as, What do we call this type of house? Who lived in teepees? What were teepees made of? Skills of eye-hand coordination, visual closure, number identification, sequencing, and vocabulary are reinforced in this activity.

Thanksgiving Patterns, page 153
More Thanksgiving Patterns, page 154

These patterns can be used in a variety of ways during the Thanksgiving season. Felt strips can be glued to figures that have been colored and cut out by the teacher for flannelboard use. These patterns can be used with Thanksgiving fingerplays (see pages 95–98). Figures can be stood up with tabs or glued to tongue depressors and used in dramatic play activities. Given duplicate patterns, children can sort them into sets and identify sets having more, less, and equal members. They can also count the number of members in each set. Children can demonstrate their understanding of one-to-one correspondence by matching a teepee for each Indian and a turkey for each Pilgrim.

Goldfish Bowl, page 155

This activity increases understanding of number concepts. This worksheet can be used when studying pets, animals, or the ocean. Children first depict water in the bowl using watercolor paints, tempera, wet chalk, or crayons. They may also enjoy drawing seaweed, rocks, or shells in the bottom of the bowl. At the top of the paper write the number of goldfish each child should place in his or her bowl. They can then draw the goldfish or paste goldfish crackers inside the bowl. Count together to see how many fish are in each bowl. Who has the most fish? Who has the fewest fish? Do any children have the same number of fish?

Calico Cat, page 156

This art project can be used when the class is studying pets. Reproduce the cat outline on construction paper (you might want to enlarge it). Help children cut out the cat. Give the children a variety of fabric scraps to cut into small pieces. Using their fingers or a paintbrush, they apply paste and place these scraps within the outline of the cat. They can add buttons for eyes, toothpicks for whiskers, and a piece of yarn for the mouth. Display cats along the windowsill.

Spot, page 157

When discussing dogs, students will enjoy making "Spot." Give children a sponge-tipped shoe polish applicator refilled with black or brown tempera paint, or a round sponge with a clothespin clipped on for easy handling and a small bowl of tempera paint. Eye-hand coordination will be built as the children paint the spots on "Spot."

Turtle Pattern, page 158

This art activity can accompany lessons on pets or nature. Reproduce turtle pattern onto cardboard or heavy paper and help the children cut it out. They may color or paint their turtles. Secure a string in the middle and take your turtles for a walk. Children also enjoy using turtles with related rhymes and fingerplays (see page 86), having turtle races, and acting out the story "The Hare and the Tortoise."

Goldfish Pattern, page 159

Children develop cutting and tracing skills as they make colorful tissue paper fish. Make a cardboard stencil at least as large as the pattern provided. Help the children trace around the fish onto double-layer tissue paper and cut out. Staple halfway around the fish. Have the children gently stuff the fish with more tissue paper. Staple around the remainder of the fish.

Have the children place a squirt of glue on each side and cover with a button or glitter for the eyes. Hang the fish together in a "school" from the ceiling with yarn.

Teddy Bear, page 160

This pattern can accompany discussions about animals, toys, or teddy bears. Skills such as fine motor coordination and concepts such as colors and counting can be learned from art projects and activities using this pattern. You can duplicate this page, or make a cardboard stencil of the bear (you might want to enlarge it). Help children trace around it onto paper and cut it out. They then paste small squares of brown tissue paper to fill in the bear. More mature children can wrap tissue paper squares around a pencil eraser, dip in glue, and fill the bear from top to bottom with "fur." The bear can also be painted with glue, sprinkled with cornmeal or coffee grounds, and decorated with button eyes. Children can name their bear, and the teacher can then write the bear's name at the bottom of the page. Using a stencil, bears can be traced onto various colors of construction paper and cut out. Have the children match and sort bears of the same color into sets, count bears, or copy color patterns using bear cutouts. Place bears in a parade line and ask, "What color bear is first, second, third, last?"

Toy Patterns, page 161

The items in this pattern can be used when studying toys or spatial relations. Glue felt strips on the back of colored and cut-out figures to use on the flannelboard. Ask the children to place the toys in directional positions, for example, "Put the teddy bear under the duck, and the drum beside the doll." Give the children a piece of paper with three lines drawn to indicate shelves. The children can color and cut out toys with assistance and glue them onto this paper following similar directions given by the teacher.

Find the Toys, page 162

Use this figure-ground perception worksheet when toys are a topic of discussion. Ask children to outline the toys, using a different color of crayon for each toy that they trace.

Together, count the number of toys in the picture.

Hand Puppet Pattern, page 163

This puppet can be made when learning about toys or when studying animals or people. An assortment of materials can be used to create a variety of characters with this pattern. Trace this pattern onto fabric or felt and help the children cut out the puppet shape. Sew or staple the puppet together. Provide children with an assortment of buttons, fabric scraps, yarn, and glue to create a doll, a person, or an animal face.

Menorah, page 164

To go along with a discussion on Hanukkah, have the children complete this worksheet. Ask them to color the flames with a yellow marker. Ask them what color of markers they would like to use to color the remainder of the picture. They can practice number skills by counting the number of flames on the Menorah.

Dreidel Pattern, page 165

This worksheet also serves as a Hanukkah-related activity. Reproduce the pattern onto cardboard or construction paper. Help the children cut out the dreidel. Stick a round toothpick through the middle, extending through the top and bottom. To play the dreidel game, give each child a pile of unshelled nuts. The children take turns spinning the dreidel like a top. If the dreidel stops with the letter "nun" at the top, the player does nothing. If it lands with "sheen" at the top, a nut is placed in the center of the table. If the dreidel lands with "hai" at the top, the player takes half of the pile of nuts. If the dreidel lands with "gimmel" at the top, the player takes all of the nuts.

Bells, Balls, Stars, and Candy Canes, page 166

Children can complete this worksheet to develop visual discrimination and fine motor skills during the Christmas season. Have the children find the ornament in each row that is different and color it green. They may color the other ornaments their favorite colors.

Christmas Stocking Pattern, page 167

Children can practice skills of cutting, tracing, and counting with this holiday activity. Make a cardboard stencil from this pattern. Help the children trace around the stencil onto double-layered red construction paper, cut out, and staple layers together to make a stocking. They can decorate the stocking with glue, glitter, and cotton balls. Hang the stockings from a classroom chimney drawn on mural paper. How many stockings are hanging on the chimney? How many students are in the classroom? Give each child a candy cane to stick in their stocking, pointing out one-to-one correspondence.

Christmas Tree, page 168

Make a stencil from this pattern for the children to trace onto green paper and cut out. Provide pieces of colorful cereal, glue, glitter, styrofoam packing balls, and pieces of foil and garland for the children to use to decorate their holiday trees.

This page can also be reproduced as a worksheet on which the children draw or glue items to decorate the tree. This open-ended art project allows room for creativity while encouraging fine motor coordination.

Ornament Patterns, page 169

These patterns can be reproduced onto construction paper or made into stencils for the children to trace and cut out. Children use creative and fine motor abilities to decorate these ornaments with glue, sequins, glitter, ribbon, sticker stars, and colored markers. Hang the ornaments with ribbon or paper clips from the ceiling or on a large tree cut from green mural paper, windows, or a real Christmas tree.

Santa Star Pattern, page 170

This Christmas activity reinforces shape recognition, tracing, cutting, and drawing skills. Make a cardboard stencil in the shape of a star. Help children trace stencil onto red construction paper and cut out. They draw features—such as a face, buttons, and belt—with black crayons or markers. They can glue on cotton balls for hands, feet, beard, and hat.

Provide stencils in triangles, rectangles, and circles and see if the children can make a different Santa shape.

Lost Toys, page 171

Use this holiday worksheet to develop visual perception and figure-ground discrimination abilities. Ask the children to find the toys that Santa has dropped and color them. Together, name the toys and then count how many toys Santa lost.

Winter Wonders, page 172

This worksheet should be used after students have had the experience of sequencing and copying patterns of holiday objects. Identify the pictures in each row of this worksheet. Help children find the pattern. Have the children cut out and paste the pictures that complete the pattern in each row. This worksheet develops skills of sequencing, visual discrimination, and eye-hand coordination.

Hats for Snowmen, page 173

Children practice cutting and pasting skills when they do this worksheet designed to reinforce the concept of one-to-one correspondence. Winter is a good time to use this worksheet. Ask the children to color the hats, cut them out, and glue one hat on each snowman's head. They may want to color the snowmen too.

Snowflake Pattern, page 174

Children use fine motor skills to make this popular winter art project. Children fold paper squares or napkins as indicated in the pattern and cut out small sections. When they unfold them, they will see that they have created beautiful snowflakes. Hang the snowflakes on the windows or from the ceiling.

Lacing Shoe Pattern, page 175

Children improve eye-hand coordination skills with this activity, which can be used when studying clothing. Use the pattern to make a cardboard shoe for each child. Help the children punch holes with a paper punch and lace with shoelace or ribbon. Mature children can be taught to tie a bow.

Mittens, page 176

During the winter or when discussing clothing items, children can do this activity. They decorate the mittens on the worksheet to look like their own mittens (or mittens they would like to have) and cut them out. String them together with yarn. Identify the colors used in each pair of mittens. If you live in a climate where children wear mittens, have them place their own mittens in a pile in the center of the floor and hang their cut-out mittens around their neck. See who can match a friend's real mittens to the ones they drew. Children build color recognition, awareness of the concept "pair," visual discrimination, and fine motor skills with this project.

Winter Clothes and Summer Clothes, page 177

This worksheet may accompany a discussion about clothing, seasons, weather, or classification of objects. If used during the winter, ask the children to color the items they wear when it snows. If used during the summer, ask them to color items they might take to the beach.

Clock and Mouse Pattern, page 178

Use this pattern with activities and discussions related to time, spatial concepts, rhyming, and opposites. Point out the top, middle, and bottom of the clock. Glue felt strips on the back of figures that have been colored and cut out, and use them on the flannelboard. Recite and illustrate the nursery rhyme "Hickory Dickory Dock." Ask the children to place a mouse on top of the clock, inside the clock, under the clock, and so on. Have children complete sentences such as "The clock is big; the mouse is _____. The hands move slow; the mouse runs _____."

Clock Lotto, page 179

Use this game to accompany discussions and lessons on telling time. Cover the game pattern with clear adhesive plastic and cut out the game board and clock lotto cards. Children use visual discrimination and fine motor skills to match and place cut-out clocks on the lotto board.

Daytime-Nighttime, page 180

This worksheet can be used when studying time concepts of day and night. Ask the children to draw something we do in the daytime under the picture of the sun and something we do at night under the moon. Children can tell you about their pictures.

Workers and Tools, page 181

Following a discussion and study of community workers and tools, children can complete this worksheet. Ask the children to cut out the tools and paste each tool beside the helper who uses the tool. Skills of visual discrimination, cutting, and pasting are reinforced while children show relationships between tools and their workers.

Chef's Hat, page 182

When studying community workers, foods, restaurants, or cooking, this pattern can be used. Help the children cut, fold, and staple the paper to make a chef's hat as directed in the pattern. Children enjoy wearing the hats for dramatic play.

Abraham Lincoln, page 183

Use this worksheet following a discussion on presidents and Abraham Lincoln. Children use fine motor skills to tear small pieces of black construction paper and paste them within the outline of Lincoln's head to make a silhouette.

Living and Nonliving Things, pages 184

This worksheet can be used following activities and discussions about living and nonliving things. Name each picture and talk about related characteristics. Help the children cut out the pictures and categorize and glue them in the appropriate column.

Safety Signs, page 185

Use these patterns during a study of safety, transportation, traffic, or street signs. Children color, cut out, and glue safety signs to popsicle sticks. They may enjoy standing up safety signs in a ball of clay and using them with vehicles in dramatic play.

Circus Patterns, page 186

Use circus patterns to accompany lessons and activities about the circus, spatial relations, numbers, and colors. Glue felt strips on the back of colored and cut-out figures and use on the flannelboard. Ask the children to place items in specific positions: the clown behind the cannon, the ball on top of the seal's nose, the monkey under the clown, and so on. You can help the children cut out the circus figures and paste them as you direct onto paper. Have the children answer questions such as, Where is the ringmaster? What color is the clown's hair? How many balls does the clown have? Reproduce multiple patterns and have the children sort them by sets and count the number of circus items in each set. Compare sets as more, less, and equal.

Elephant Parade, page 187

This worksheet can reinforce knowledge about ordinal numbers, colors, and sequence when the children are learning about the circus. Direct them to color the blanket of the first elephant blue, the second pink, the third red, and the last one yellow. They can color the remainder of the picture as they wish. Ask them to tell you which colors they used in their pictures.

Balloons for the Clown, page 188

Use this worksheet when learning about the circus, colors, or shapes. Have the children draw balloons for the clown. Ask them to name the shapes and colors of their balloons. Count together how many balloons the clown is holding. Children can color the clown with their crayons or bright markers.

Lucky Charms, page 189

These patterns can be duplicated, colored, cut out, and used in a variety of ways. Strips of felt can be glued on the backs for flannelboard use, or they can be duplicated and covered with clear adhesive plastic to use for sorting, classifying, and sequencing activities. Demonstrate a sequence and see if the children can name the shape that would come next. Review the names and colors of each shape. Children can color the shapes with crayons or markers.

Help them cut out the shapes and hang them from a hanger or a stick to make a mobile.

Shamrock Pattern, page 190

Reproduce the pattern onto sturdy green paper. Help the children cut out the St. Patrick's Day shamrock and punch holes around the outer edge. They then develop eye-hand coordination skills by lacing the shamrock with their favorite color of yarn. Fasten a small piece of tape at the end of the yarn for easier threading.

Irish Flag, page 191

St. Patrick's week is a good time to make an Irish flag. Children should be encouraged to color from left to right in green, white, and orange. They then cut out and staple their flags to straws. The children may enjoy marching in a parade with their flags.

Three-Heart Shamrock, page 192

Use this worksheet when learning about shapes or during St. Patrick's week. Help the children cut out the hearts and glue them together with a stem to make a shamrock. They can cover their shamrock with small squares of green tissue paper or cellophane.

Dot-to-Dot Food, page 193

Use this worksheet with activities and discussions relating to food and nutrition. Have the children trace the dotted lines to complete the pictures of common foods and color them their natural colors. Ask the children to name the foods and their respective colors. Visual perception, fine motor coordination skills, and color identification are reinforced by this activity.

Follow the Path, page 194

Use this worksheet to accompany a discussion of where food comes from. Children use eye-hand coordination abilities to follow a maze from the food to its source.

Button Bunny, page 195

This pattern can be used to teach number concepts or colors during Easter holiday activities. Reproduce the bunny onto various colors of construction paper, write a different number on each bow tie, and cover with clear adhesive plastic. Hide bunnies throughout the room for the children to hunt for. Ask the children to identify each bunny's color and number. They place correct number of buttons on the bunny's tummy. Line up the bunnies in order from least to most buttons.

This can also be used as a worksheet on which the children draw the designated number of buttons on the bunny.

Giant Easter Egg, page 196

Use this art activity during the Easter season to encourage fine motor development and creativity. Have the children color designs with crayons and then paint the eggs with diluted tempera. Help them cut out their eggs when dry. Display them on a glass-colored mural or the classroom windows. Ribbons, sequins, stickers, and other decorative items can also be glued to the egg to create an Easter egg collage.

Bunny Headband, page 197

Children will enjoy making bunny headbands during the Easter season. Skills of cutting, coloring, and pasting are reinforced as the children follow this pattern. Give them ears to cut out and color, and cotton balls to paste around the edge of each ear. Staple ears to the back of a 2-inch headband that fits around the child's head. Children enjoy wearing their hats and doing the Bunny Hop together.

Easter Eggs, page 198

Skills of visual discrimination, eye-hand coordination, and sequence are stimulated in this Easter activity. Give children this worksheet and ask them to cut out the eggs at the bottom of the page and paste each egg in the correct row to follow a pattern. They can color the eggs bright colors.

Baby Animals, page 199

This pattern may be duplicated, colored, cut out, and used in a variety of ways to reinforce numerical concepts or accompany a discussion about baby animals. Prepare the pattern for a flannelboard, or reproduce it and cover the pictures with clear adhesive plastic to use as a demonstration aid. Children can also color and cut out these baby animals. Direct them to place animals in a row from left to right: "First put the lamb. The second animal will be a cat." They can then place numbers in a row, matching one numeral for each animal. Count the animals together. Place sets of animals on the flannelboard or the floor, and have the children count them and find the corresponding numeral. Help the children compare sets as more, less, and equal.

Rattles for Babies, page 200

Use this worksheet to accompany a discussion of babies or one-to-one correspondence. Children will demonstrate awareness of one-to-one correspondence and fine motor abilities by drawing a rattle for each baby.

Baby's Diaper, page 201

This worksheet can accompany a discussion about babies; it develops cutting and drawing skills. Have the children cut out a diaper from a piece of cloth and paste it on the baby. They can then draw facial features and a toy for the baby.

Cow Pattern, page 202

When studying the farm or animals, you can give the children this pattern, which has been traced or copied onto construction paper. Have them paste small pieces of black or brown crushed tissue paper onto the cow. They can draw a green pasture for the cow.

Pig Pattern, page 203

This pattern can be used when studying animals or the farm. Make a stencil and help the children trace the pig onto pink construction paper and cut it out. They paint mud on another paper, using brown shoe polish with a sponge applicator or brown tempera paint. They paste the pig in the mud and add a twist tie for a tail. Fine motor abilities are developed with this art activity.

Corn for the Chickens, page 204

Children develop fine motor skills in this animal-related activity as they glue corn kernels along the line to connect the hen to her baby chicks. They can also trace the line with a pencil or crayon.

Hidden Butterflies and Caterpillars, page 205

Use this figure-ground discrimination worksheet to accompany a discussion about butterflies or nature. Have the children find the hidden butterflies and caterpillars and draw a ring around each one. Count together how many each child found. Have the children color the picture.

From Tadpole to Frog, page 206

During a study of nature, reproduction, or animals, the children can complete this worksheet. Review the stages of a frog, and help the students cut out the pictures and place them in proper sequence. Then have the children paste these pictures showing the stages of a frog's development on another sheet of paper.

Wheels, page 207

This worksheet can accompany a discussion about transportation, vehicles, or shapes. Children demonstrate fine motor abilities by tracing the dotted lines to draw the wheels on each vehicle. They then color the vehicles. Ask the children to count the number of wheels on each picture and name the vehicles on the worksheet.

Train and Engineer, page 208

Use this pattern as a worksheet to accompany a discussion on transportation. Have the children color the train and draw someone riding in the window.

Visual perception abilities can be developed if the teacher cuts a hole in the train window and gradually exposes a child's picture in the window while the children try to guess whose picture it is.

This pattern can also be reproduced on construction paper and given as a present. Help the children cut out the train and glue their picture in the window. They can color the train and give it to someone special as a gift.

Space Shapes, page 209

This worksheet may accompany a discussion about space, patterns, or shapes. Ask the children to identify which shape would come next in each row. They complete the pattern by drawing the appropriate shape, demonstrating fine motor and sequencing skills.

Counting Animals, page 210

Use this worksheet to reinforce numerical concepts when studying animals. Have children count the number of animals in each box and circle the corresponding numeral. They can name and color the animals in each box.

Animal Homes, page 211

Use this worksheet with activities and discussions about animals or animal homes. Talk about the pictures in the boxes and the animals at the bottom of the page. Help the children cut out the animals and paste them in their habitats. Children can then color the animals and their habitats. Children develop fine motor skills while demonstrating an understanding of science concepts.

Handprints, page 212

This activity makes a nice remembrance for parents to save. Help children dip their hands in mud or paint and place on each side of the poem to make handprints. The child or the teacher can write the child's name at the top of the page.

Dinosaur and Leaves Pattern, page 213

This activity accompanies the study of dinosaurs. Make a stencil for the children to trace and cut out. Write a numeral on each dinosaur, and have the children cut out the correct number of leaves to give their dinosaur.

The teacher can also color, cut out, and use this pattern on a flannelboard by gluing felt strips on the back of each dinosaur.

Dinosaurs can be hidden in the classroom for children to hunt. When they find a dinosaur, they identify the number on it and give it the proper number of leaves to eat.

Tyrannosaurus Rex Puppet, page 214

This activity may accompany a dinosaur lesson. Reproduce the pattern onto green construction paper. Help the children cut out the head of the dinosaur and connect the jaws with a paper fastener. They can color features with crayons. Fine motor abilities are enhanced when the children make this puppet.

Dot-to-Dot Stegosaurus, page 215

This activity is useful with a discussion of dinosaurs. Children improve visual perception and eye-hand coordination skills by tracing the dotted line to complete the dinosaur picture. They then paint the Stegosaurus with glue and cover with cornflakes to give a "spiky" appearance.

Counting Coins, page 216

Use this worksheet with activities and discussions related to money and counting coins. Numerical abilities and fine motor skills are enhanced with this activity. Provide the children with real quarters, nickels, dimes, and pennies. They can place coins on outlines and count the number of coins in each row. Or they can cut and paste the numeral that corresponds to the set of coins in each row. Mature students may be asked instead to write the numerals that correspond to the coins in each row.

The children can also be asked to sort coins into sets and then identify the kind of coin in each set and count the number of coins in each set. They can also sequence coins in order of size, from smallest to largest. Tell the children that size does not match the value of the coins.

Pinwheels, page 217

This project may accompany a discussion about wind, air, or movement. Children develop fine motor skills by cutting out the square and along the dotted lines in the pattern. Help them fold Corners 1, 2, 3, and 4 to the center and tack to a dowel or pencil eraser. The children can blow the pinwheels or take them outside in the wind and observe the movement caused by air.

Unfinished Birthday Cake, page 218

This worksheet may accompany a discussion or celebration of birthdays or "unbirthdays" throughout the school year. Fine motor and counting skills are developed as the children draw the number of candles that equal their age and color the cake. Count the number of candles on each cake and discuss who is the oldest and who is the youngest in the class. Children enjoy singing " Happy Birthday" when classmates have a birthday to celebrate.

Name _____

 # The Schoolbus

Color the bus and the wheels.
Cut out the wheels and paste them on the bus.

✎ My Mirror ✎

Draw your face in the mirror. Color your picture.

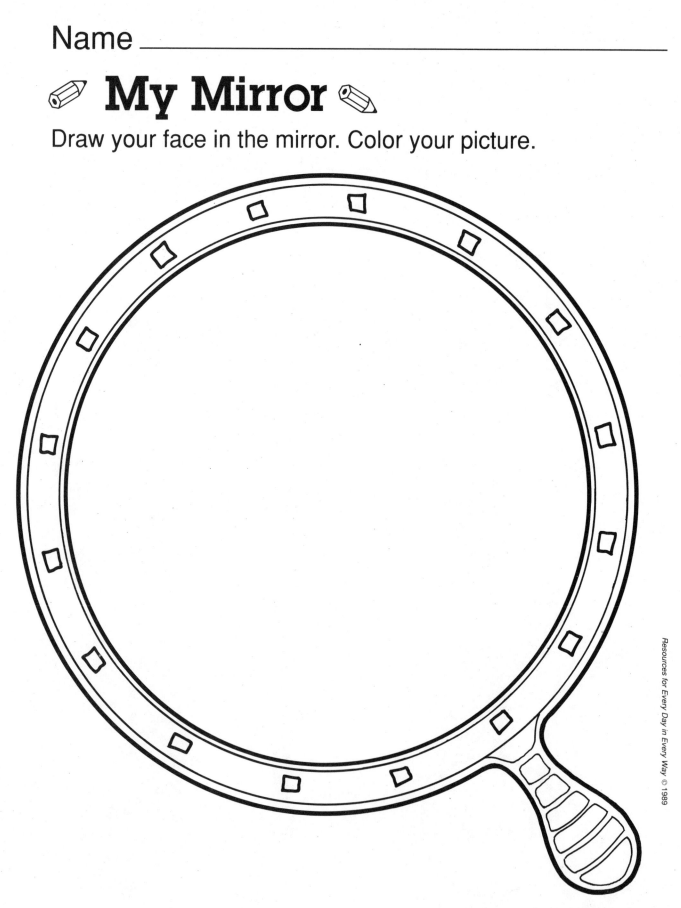

Resources for Every Day in Every Way © 1989

Name _____

 # What's Missing?

Complete the picture. Color it.

Name _____

✎ What's Missing? ✎

Complete the picture. Color it.

Resources for Every Day in Every Way © 1989

Name _____

✎ On, Under, Next To, and In Front Of ✎

Color, cut out, and paste on another piece of paper.

Fingerpuppets with Feelings ✎

Color and cut out. Tape around fingers.

Happy

Sad

Scared

Angry

Sleepy

Resources for Every Day in Every Way © 1989

Name _____

✏ **Weather Chart** ✏

Month _____ Day _____ Year _____

	Monday	Tuesday	Wednesday	Thursday	Friday
Temperature					
Wind					
Clouds					
Precipitation					

✏️ Weather Pictures ✏️

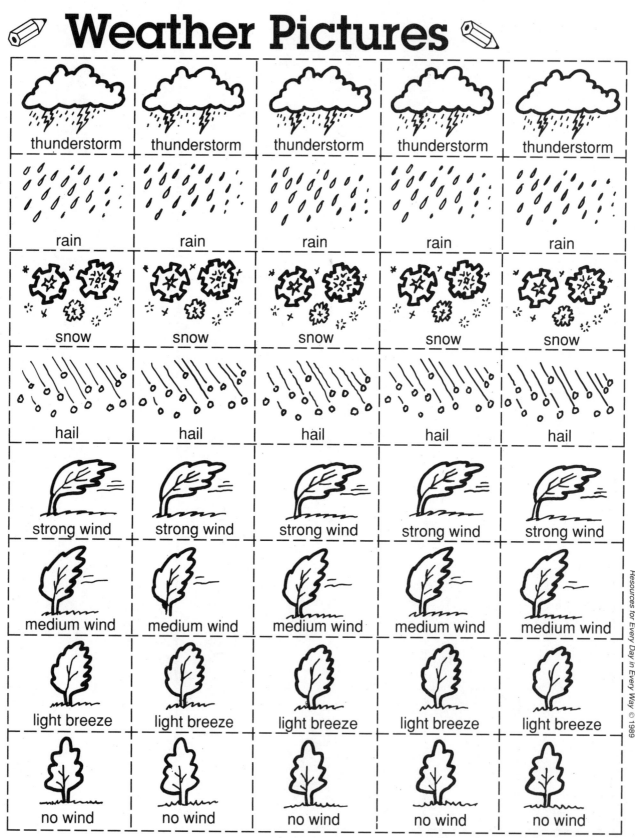

thunderstorm	thunderstorm	thunderstorm	thunderstorm	thunderstorm
rain	rain	rain	rain	rain
snow	snow	snow	snow	snow
hail	hail	hail	hail	hail
strong wind	strong wind	strong wind	strong wind	strong wind
medium wind	medium wind	medium wind	medium wind	medium wind
light breeze	light breeze	light breeze	light breeze	light breeze
no wind	no wind	no wind	no wind	no wind

Resources for Every Day in Every Way © 1989

Resources for Every Day in Every Way

Name _____

✎ More Weather Pictures ✎

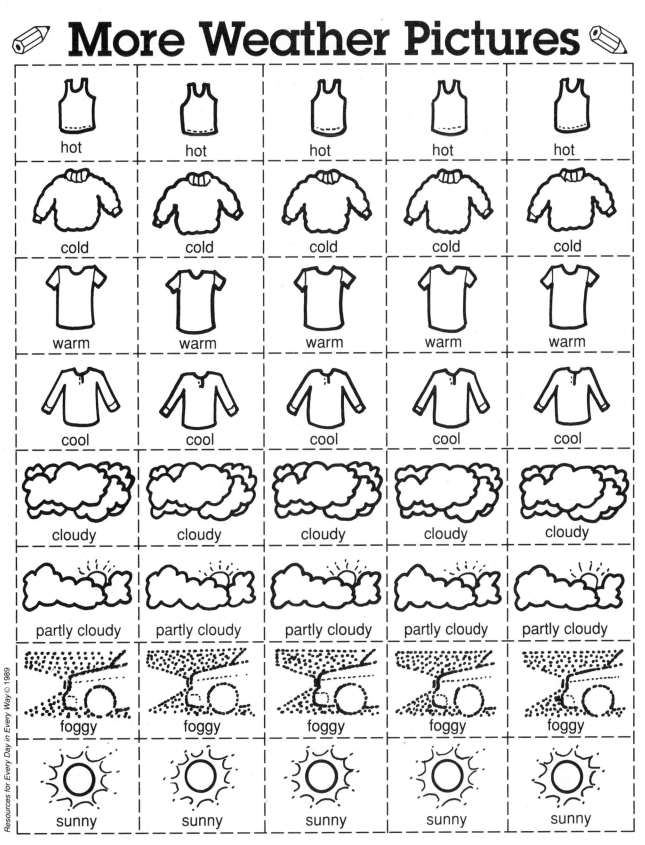

hot	hot	hot	hot	hot
cold	cold	cold	cold	cold
warm	warm	warm	warm	warm
cool	cool	cool	cool	cool
cloudy	cloudy	cloudy	cloudy	cloudy
partly cloudy	partly cloudy	partly cloudy	partly cloudy	partly cloudy
foggy	foggy	foggy	foggy	foggy
sunny	sunny	sunny	sunny	sunny

Name _____

✏ Fall Favorites ✏

Which are the same?
Color the matching pictures in each row.

Resources for Every Day in Every Way

✏ Hidden Halloween Ghosts ✎

How many ghosts are hiding in this picture? Draw a ring around each ghost. Color the picture.

Shape-a-Picture ✎

Color and cut out shapes. Paste together to create pictures.

Halloween Patterns

Color and cut out.

More Halloween Patterns

Color and cut out.

✐ Bat Pattern ✐

Materials

Art paper 6" X 18" black
Two egg carton sections
Pencil and eraser
Scissors and paste

Procedure

1. Fold 6" X 18" in half to 6" X 9". Trace and cut out bat pattern. (Fig. A)
2. Paste on egg carton eyes.
3. Cut out 1/2" diameter black art paper eyes. Paste cutouts in center of each egg carton section. (Fig. B)
4. Cut small circle of red and orange for bat's nose.

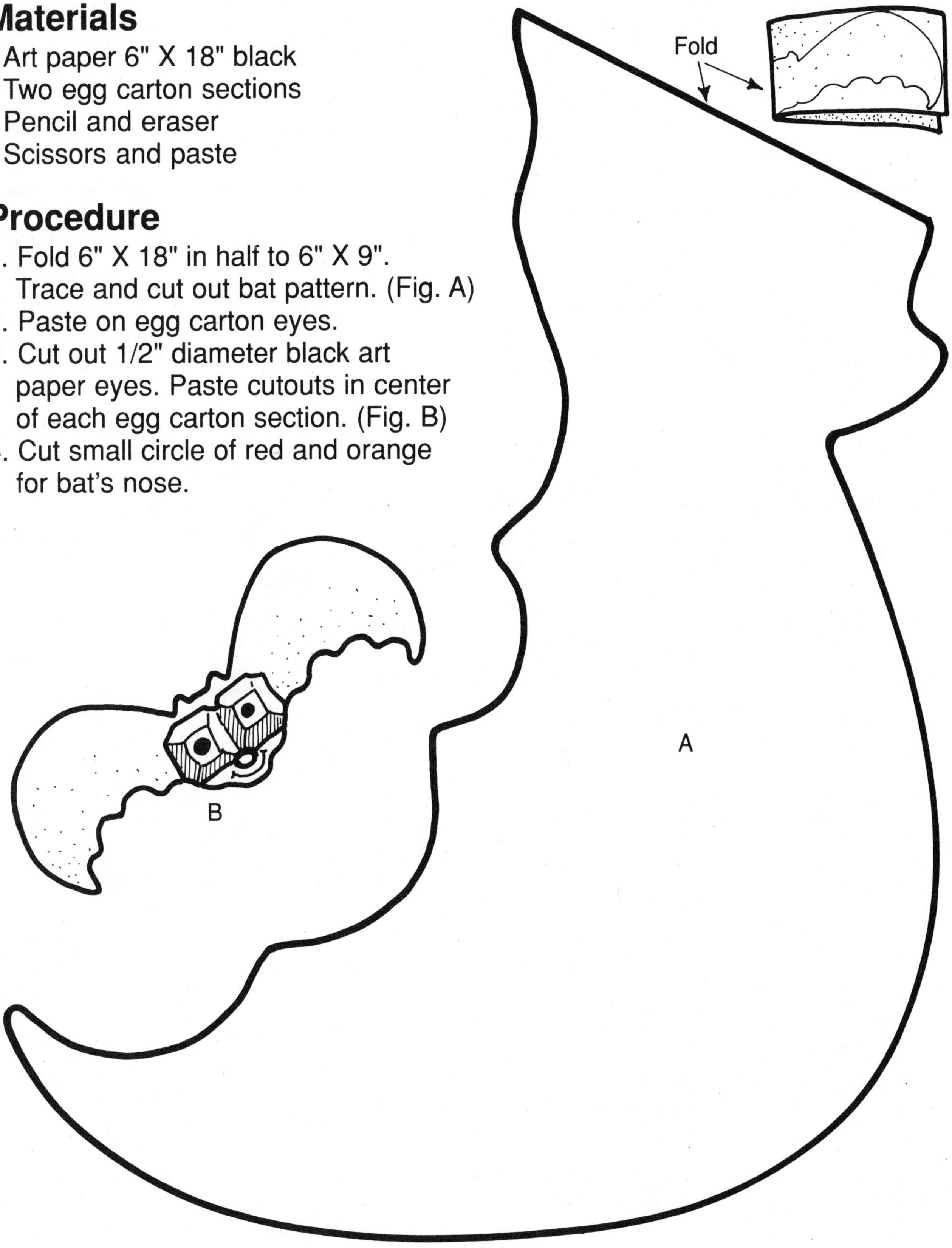

Fold

A

B

Name_____

 # Brother to Sister Maze, #1

Help brother find sister. Draw a line along the path.

Brother

Sister

Name _____

✏️ Sister to Brother Maze, #2 ✏️

Help sister find brother. Draw a line along the path.

Sister

Brother

Name _____

 # Family Members

Color and cut out.

Resources for Every Day in Every Way

House Pattern

Color and cut out.

✏ Certificates ✏

Color and cut out.

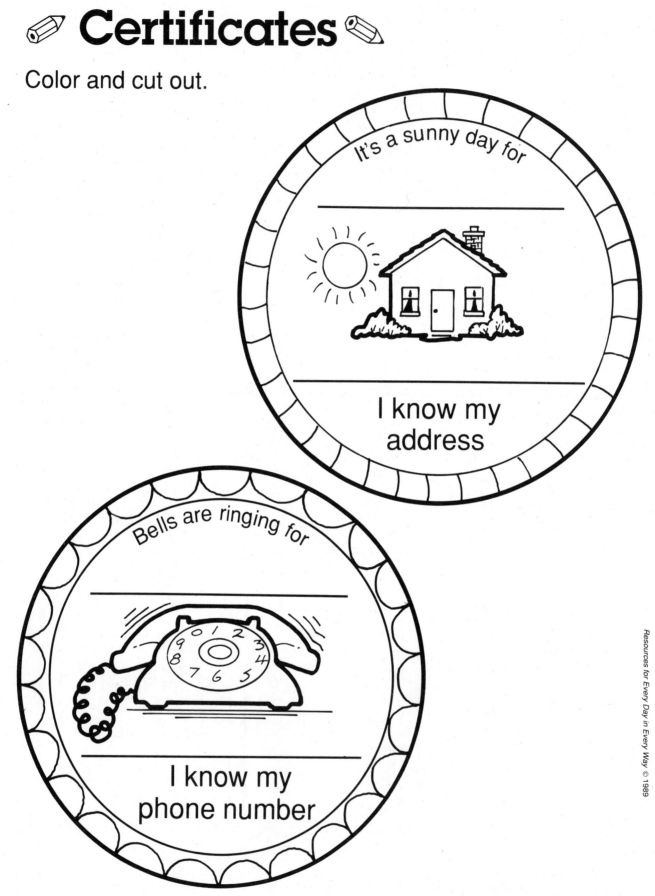

It's a sunny day for

I know my
address

Bells are ringing for

I know my
phone number

Name _____

Complete the Houses

Make the houses in each row look the same.
Draw the missing shape in the second house.

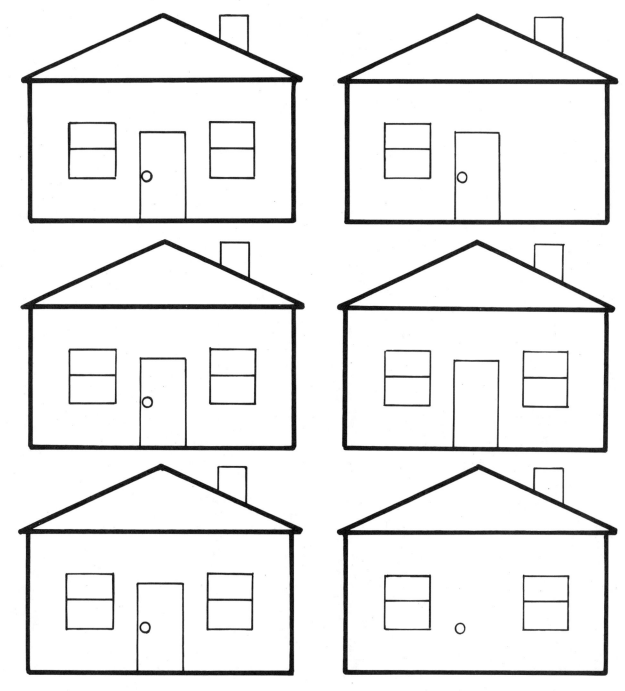

Name _____

✏ Dot-to-Dot Teepee ✏

Start with number 1 and connect the dots to complete the picture. Color the picture.

✏️ Thanksgiving Patterns ✏️

Color and cut out.

✏ More Thanksgiving Patterns ✏

Color and cut out.

✐ Goldfish Bowl ✎

Paint or draw water in the bowl.
Draw some seaweed. Add goldfish.

Calico Cat

Paste fabric scraps on the cat.

Resources for Every Day in Every Way © 1989

Name _____

 # Spot

Paint spots on the dog.

Turtle Pattern

Reproduce on cardboard. Color and cut out. Thread and knot a piece of string through the hole in the middle of the shell.

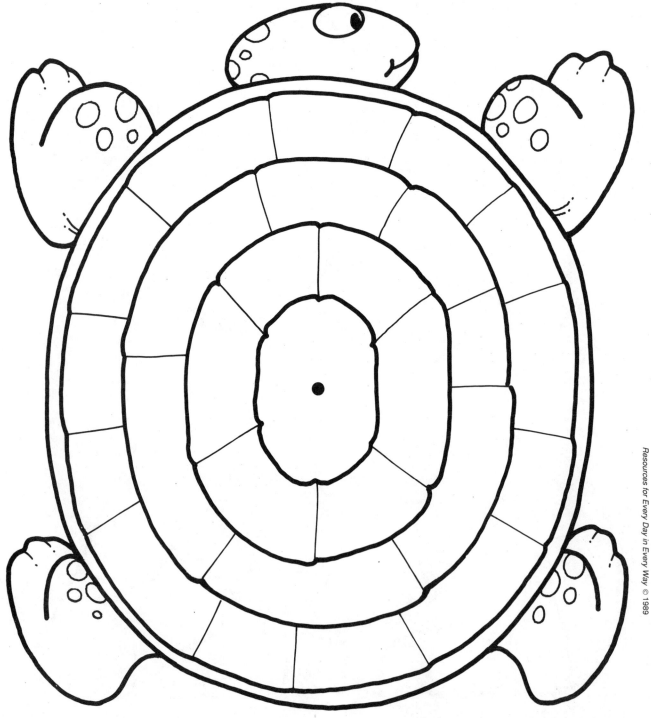

Resources for Every Day in Every Way

Resources for Every Day in Every Way © 1989

✏️ Goldfish Pattern ✏️

Make a cardboard stencil. Trace onto two layers of tissue paper. Stuff with tissue paper and staple together.

Name _____

🖉 Teddy Bear 🖉

Paste brown tissue paper squares on the teddy bear.

Teddy Bear's Name _____

Resources for Every Day in Every Way

Toy Patterns

Color and cut out.

Resources for Every Day in Every Way © 1989

Name _____

✏ Find the Toys ✏

Outline each toy with different color of crayon.

Resources for Every Day in Every Way © 1989

✏️ Hand Puppet Pattern ✏️

Cut pattern on two layers of fabric. Sew or staple together. Decorate with buttons, yarn, and fabric scraps.

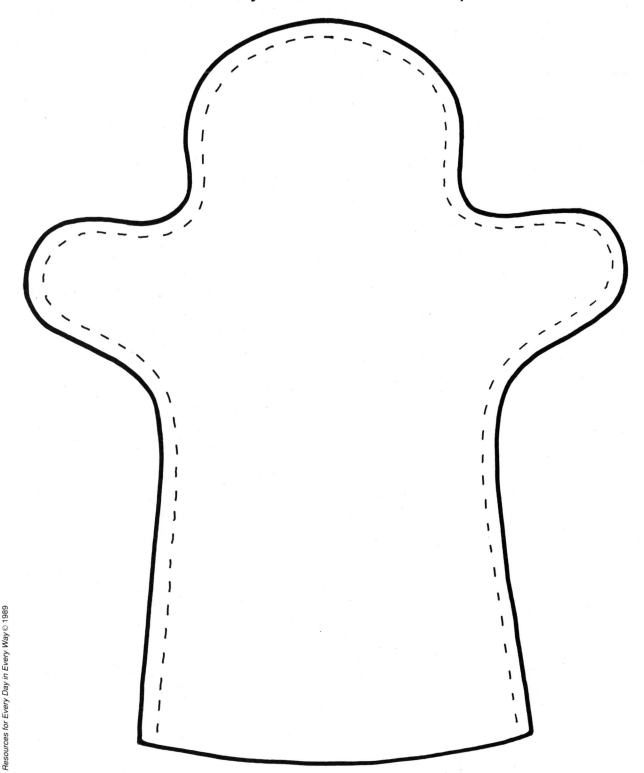

Name _____

 # Menorah

Color the flames with a yellow marker.

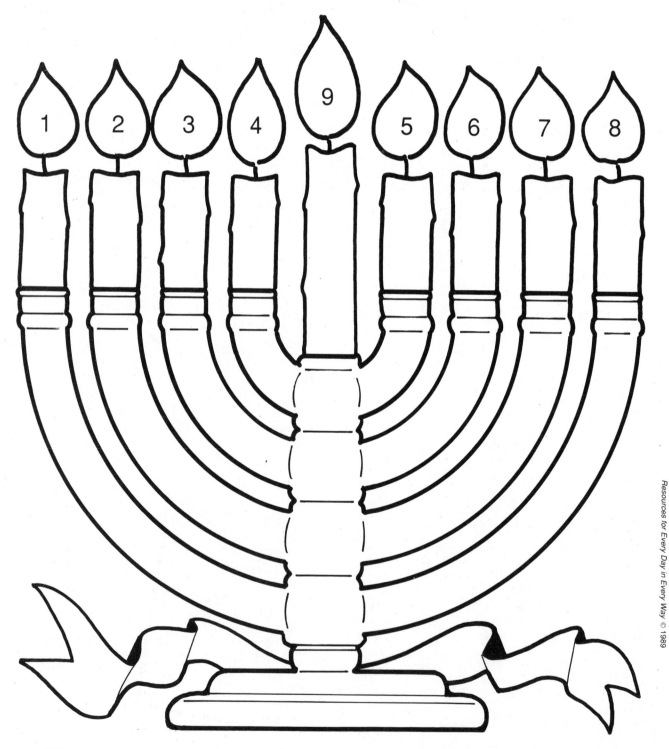

Resources for Every Day in Every Way

✏️ Dreidel Pattern ✏️

Cut out circle. Put round toothpick through the center.

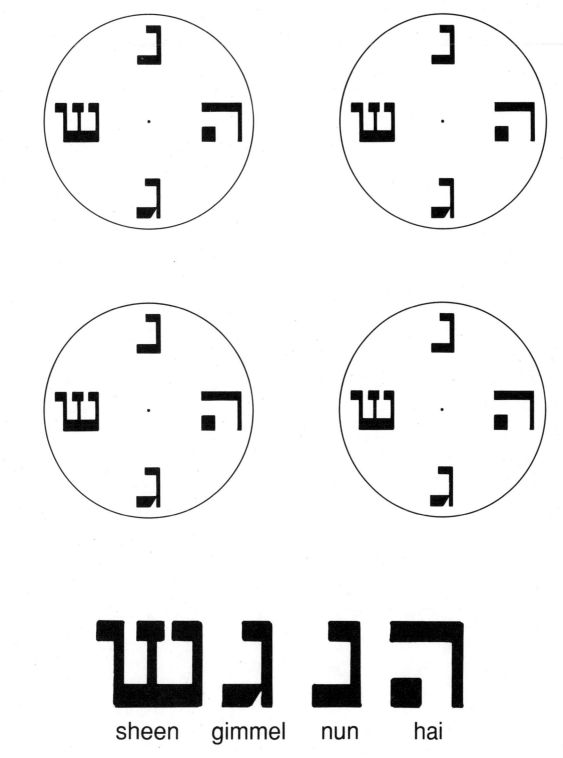

sheen   gimmel   nun   hai

Resources for Every Day in Every Way © 1989

Bells, Balls, Stars, and Candy Canes

Find the ornament that is different in each row. Color it green.

Resources for Every Day in Every Way © 1989

✎ Christmas Stocking Pattern✎

Cut out two, staple, and decorate.

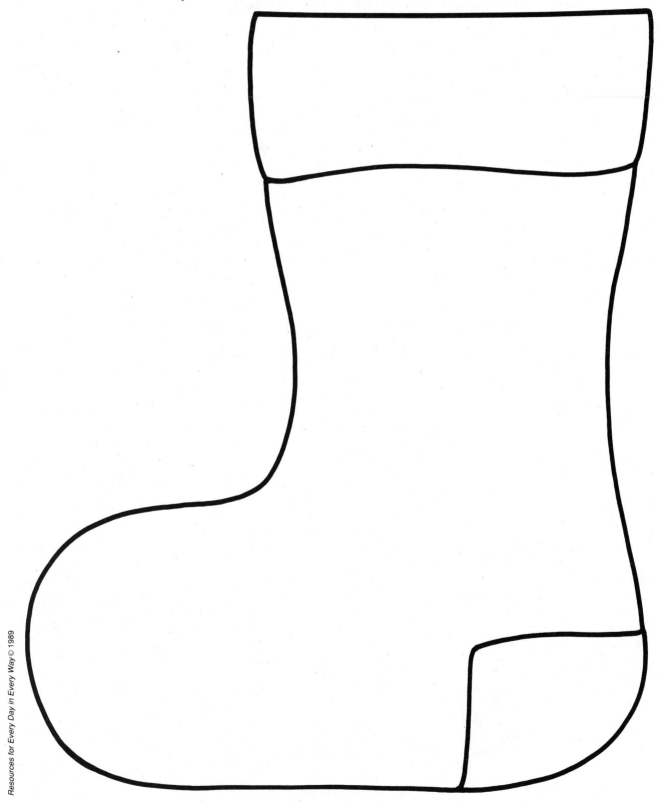

Name _____

 # Christmas Tree

Decorate the tree.

✏️ Ornament Patterns ✏️

Color, cut out, and decorate.

✏️ Santa Star Pattern ✏️

Make a stencil and trace onto red construction paper. Cut out and draw features in black. Glue on cotton balls for hands, feet, beard, and hat.

Name_____

 # Lost Toys

What toys did Santa drop? Color each toy. Count them.

Winter Wonders

Cut out the pictures at the bottom of the page.
Paste on the one that completes each pattern.

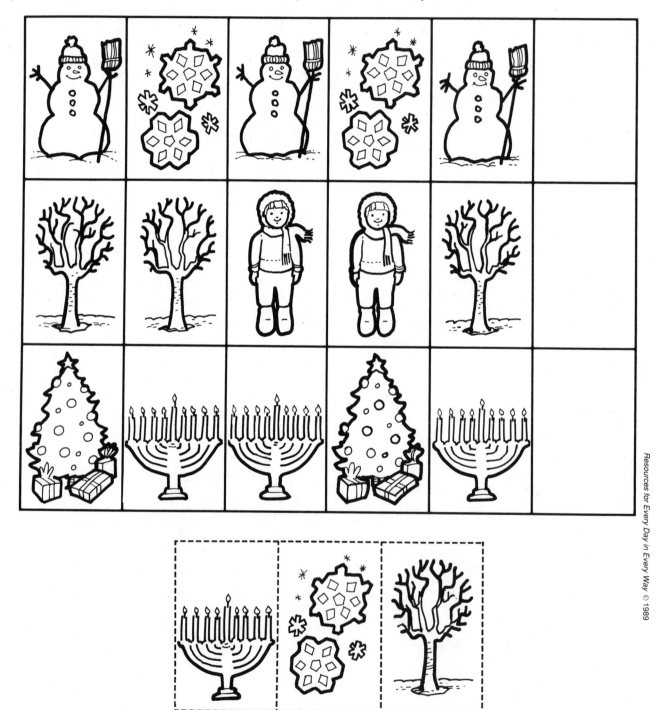

Resources for Every Day in Every Way © 1989

Name _____

Hats for Snowmen

Color and cut out hats. Paste one hat on each snowman.

Snowflake Pattern

1. Take a napkin, folded in square as it comes from the package.
2. Fold napkin into triangle.
3. Fold bottom point up to meet the top point.
4. Cut out small sections.
5. Open and view snowflake.

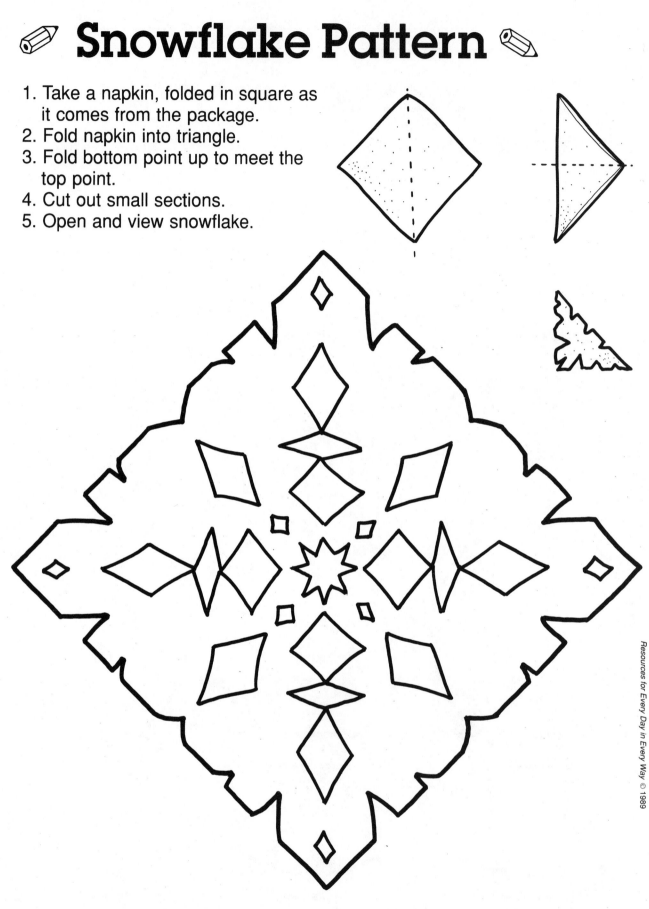

Resources for Every Day in Every Way © 1989

Lacing Shoe Pattern

Cut out and punch holes.
Lace a shoelace or ribbon through the holes.

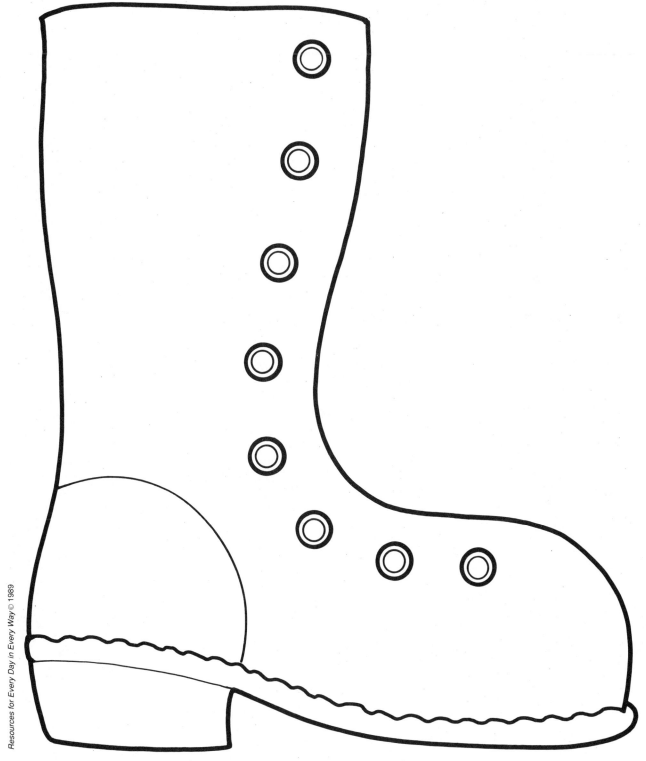

Name _____

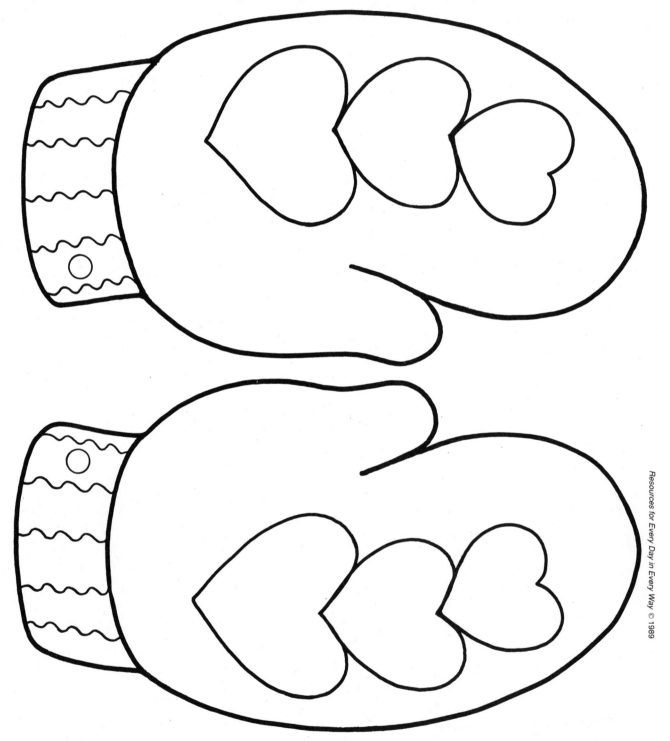 Mittens ✏️

Color and cut out the mittens. String together with yarn.

✏ Winter Clothes and Summer Clothes ✐

Which clothes are for winter? Which items are for the beach? Color as directed.

  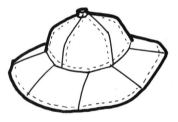

✏ Clock and Mouse Pattern✏

Color and cut out for flannelboard.

Clock Lotto ✏️

Cut out gameboard and cards.
Match the cards to the clocks on the gameboard.

Gameboard   ## Lotto Cards

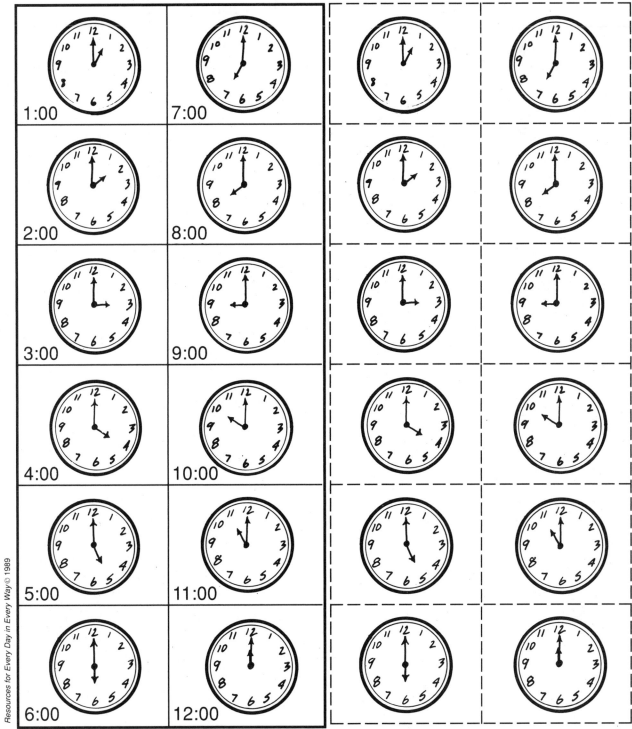

Resources for Every Day in Every Way © 1989

Name _____

 Daytime-Nighttime ✏️

What do we do in the daytime? Draw a picture under the sun.
What do we do at night? Draw a picture under the moon.

Daytime　　　　　　　　　**Nighttime**

Name _____

✏ Workers and Tools ✏

Cut out the tool cards. Paste each card beside the worker who uses that tool.

police officer

firefighter

letter carrier

teacher

dentist

baker

Resources for Every Day in Every Way © 1989

Chef's Hat

From a piece of 17" X 24" white tissue paper, the children cut two 4"-wide strips and a large circle. The strips are folded in half, stapled together, and then fit around each child's head; staple the ends of the band together. The circle is widely fringed, as shown in the diagram, and glued or stapled to the headband.

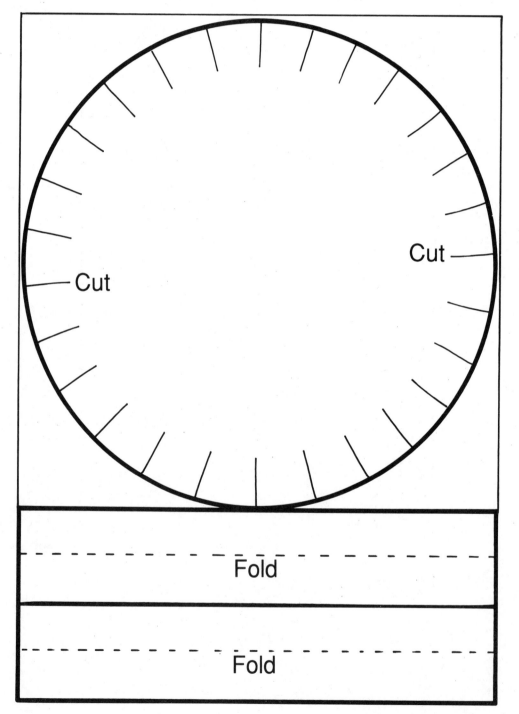

Resources for Every Day in Every Way © 1989 I

Name _____

 # Abraham Lincoln ✏️

Tear small pieces of black paper. Paste inside outline.

Name _____

 # Living and Nonliving Things

Cut out the pictures. Paste those that are living under the tree. Paste nonliving things under the chair.

living   nonliving

Resources for Every Day in Every Way © 1989

Resources for Every Day in Every Way

Name _____

✎ Safety Signs ✎

Color and cut out safety signs. Glue onto popsicle sticks.

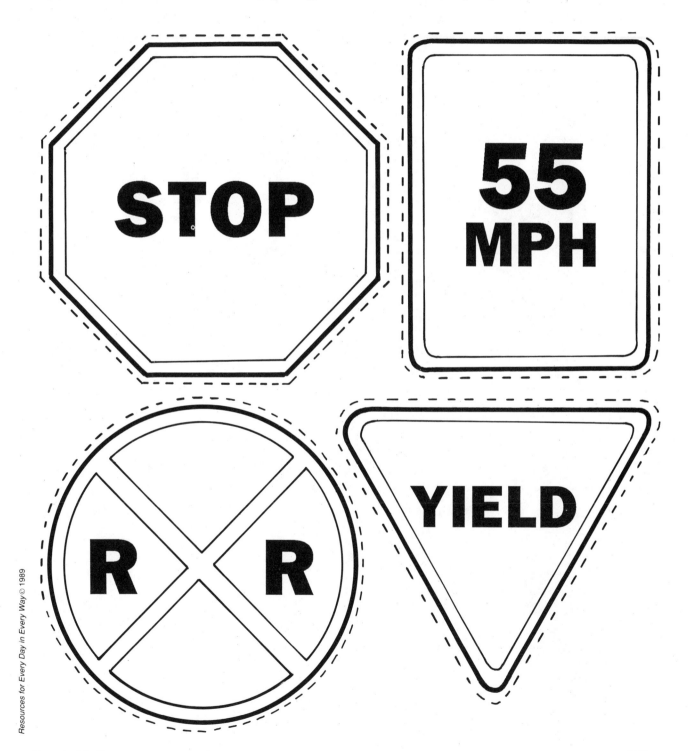

STOP

55 MPH

R R

YIELD

Circus Patterns

Color and cut out.

Resources for Every Day in Every Way © 1989

Name _____

✏ Elephant Parade ✏

Color the blanket of the first elephant blue, the second pink, the third red, and the last one yellow. Finish coloring the picture.

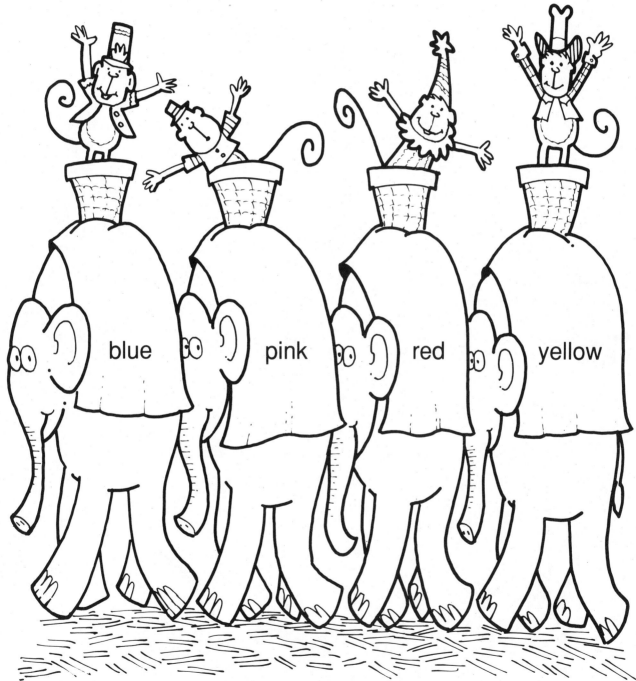

blue   pink   red   yellow

 Balloons for the Clown

Draw balloons for the clown. Color the balloons and the clown.

Resources for Every Day in Every Way © 1989

Name _____

 # Lucky Charms

Color and cut out the shapes.

✏️ Shamrock Pattern ✏️

Reproduce on heavy green paper.
Cut out and punch holes around edges for lacing.

Name_____

 # Irish Flag

Color and cut out flag. Staple onto a straw.

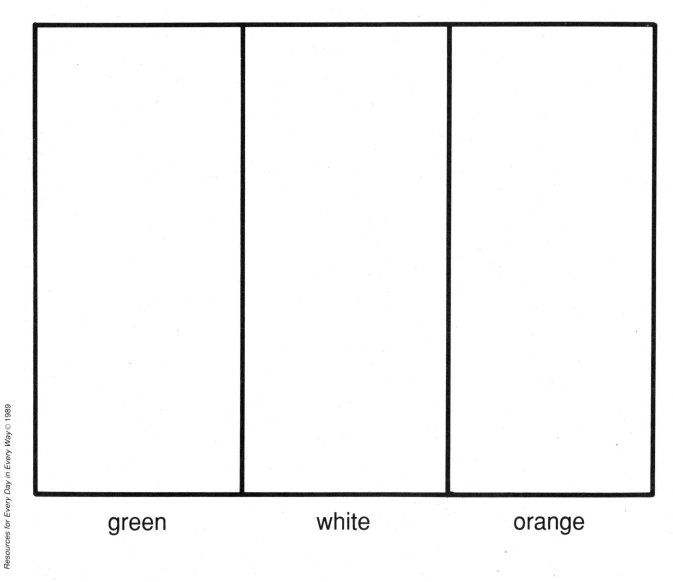

| green | white | orange |

 Three-Heart Shamrock ✏️

Cut out three hearts and staple or glue together with stem to make a shamrock. Cover with small pieces of green tissue paper or cellophane.

stem

Resources for Every Day in Every Way

✏ Dot-to-Dot Food ✏

Trace the dotted lines to complete the pictures. Color the foods.

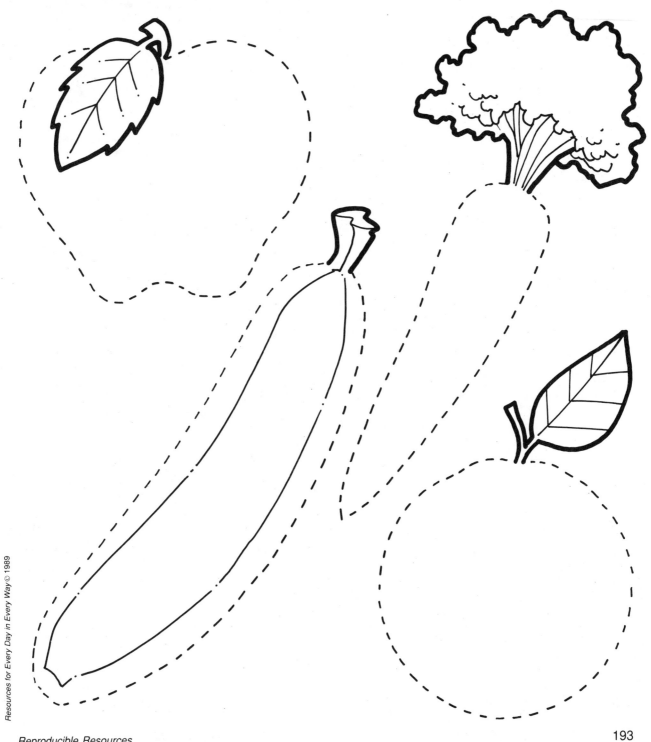

Follow the Path

Follow the path with your pencil.

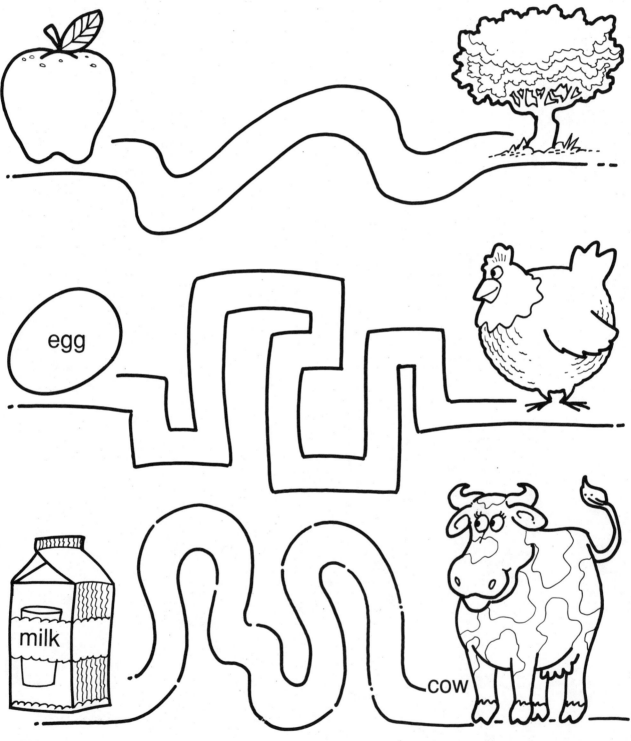

Resources for Every Day in Every Way © 1989

Name _____

 # Button Bunny

Give the bunny some buttons.

Bunny's Name _____   Number of Buttons_____

✐ Giant Easter Egg ✐

Color designs on the egg; and cut it out.

Bunny Headband

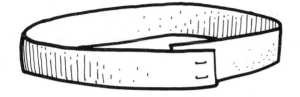

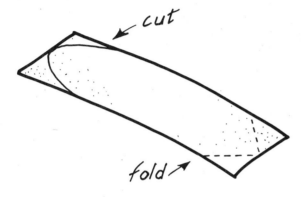

Staple a 2" X 24" strip of construction paper to fit head.

Children cut out two ears from 12" X 3" strips of white construction paper and color them pink. Then they fold the bottom corners to the center.

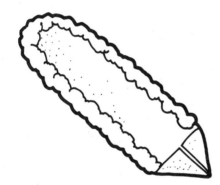

Children paste cotton balls around edge of ears.

Staple ears onto headband.

Name _____

✐ Easter Eggs ✐

Cut out the eggs at the bottom of the page. Paste one in each row to complete the pattern. Color the eggs bright colors.

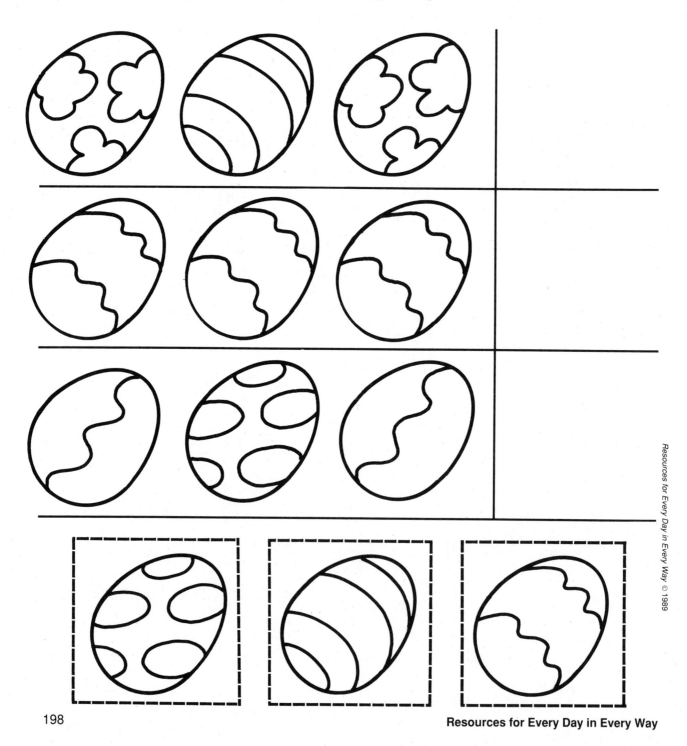

Resources for Every Day in Every Way

Name _____

Baby Animals

Color and cut out. Place animals in a row and number them.

1   3

2   4

5

✏️ Rattles for Babies ✏️

Draw a rattle for each baby.

Name

✏ Baby's Diaper ✏

Paste a diaper on baby. Draw a face on the baby. Draw a toy for it.

Reproducible Resources

Name _____

 Cow Pattern

Paste tissue paper on the cow. Make a green pasture for it.

Name _____

Cut out and paste on brown paper. Add a twist tie for the tail.

Name _____

✏ Corn for the Chickens ✎

Help the hen feed the baby chicks. Glue kernels of corn along the line. Color the hen and her chicks.

Name _____

✐ Hidden Butterflies and Caterpillars ✐

How many butterflies and caterpillars are hiding in the picture? Draw a ring around each one. Color the picture.

Name _____

From Tadpole to Frog

Color and cut out the pictures. Which stage comes first?
Which comes next? Glue them in order.

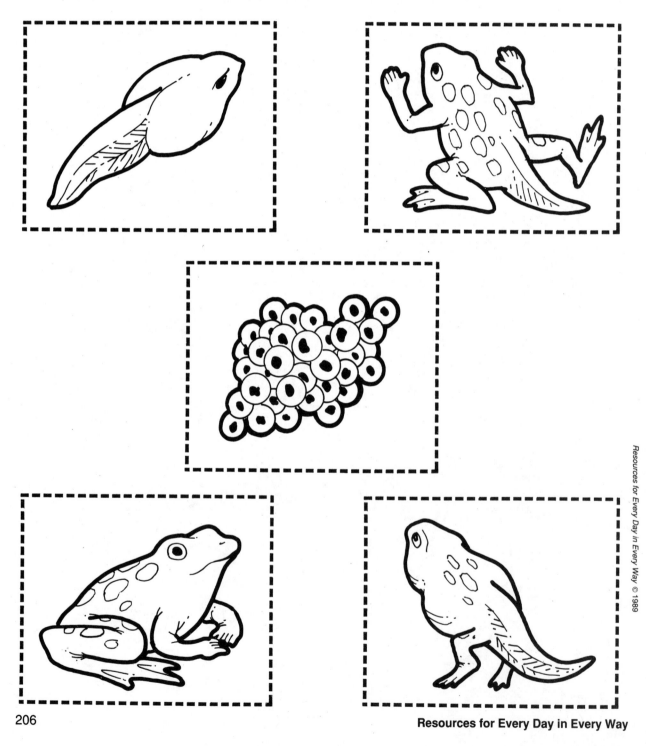

Resources for Every Day in Every Way

Name

✏ Wheels ✏

Trace the dotted line to complete each item. Color the pictures.

Name _____

Train and Engineer

Color the train.

Name _____

✏️ **Space Shapes** ✏️

What is the pattern? Draw the space shape that comes next in each row.

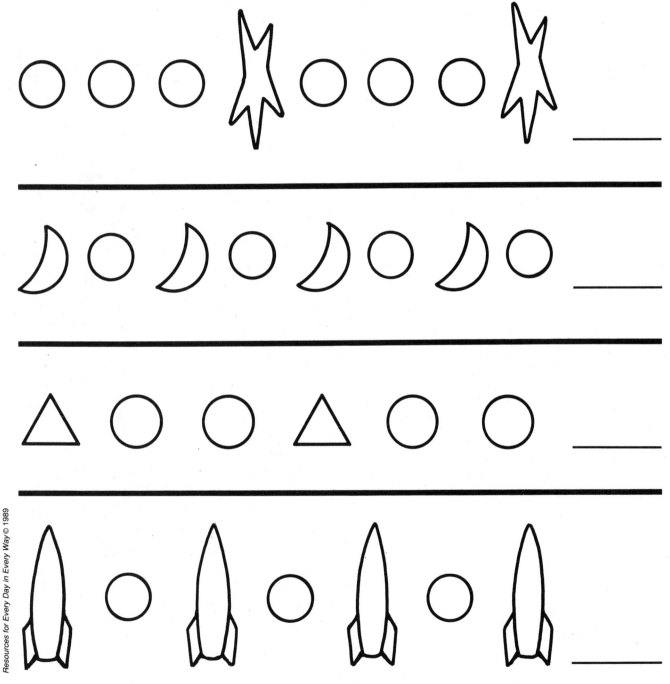

Resources for Every Day in Every Way © 1989

Name_____

✏ Counting Animals ✏

Count the number of animals in each box. Draw a ring around the number of animals in each box.

Name _____

✏ **Animal Homes** ✏

Cut out the animals. Paste each animal in the box that
shows where it lives.

Name _____

Handprints

Sometimes you get discouraged
Because I am so small
And always leave my fingerprints
On furniture and walls.

But every day I'm growing—
I'll be grown up someday—
And all those tiny handprints
Will surely fade away.

So here's a final handprint
Just so you can recall
Exactly how my fingers looked
When I was very small.

Dinosaur and Leaves Pattern ✎

Color and cut out.

Name _____

 Tyrannosaurus Rex Puppet

Color and cut out. Connect jaws with a paper fastener.

Resources for Every Day in Every Way © 1989

✎ Dot-to-Dot Stegosaurus ✎

Trace the dotted line to complete the dinosaur.

Name _____

✏️ Counting Coins ✏️

Cut out numbers and paste them by the rows of coins to show the number in each row.

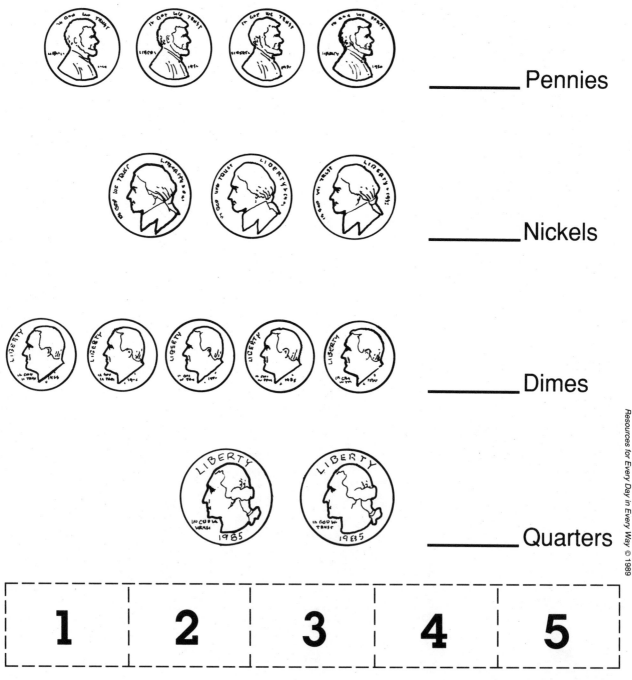

_____ Pennies

_____ Nickels

_____ Dimes

_____ Quarters

| 1 | 2 | 3 | 4 | 5 |

Resources for Every Day in Every Way © 1989

 **Pinwheel**

Cut out large square. Cut along dotted lines. Fold corners 1, 2, 3, and 4 to center. Attach to a pencil with a thumb tack.

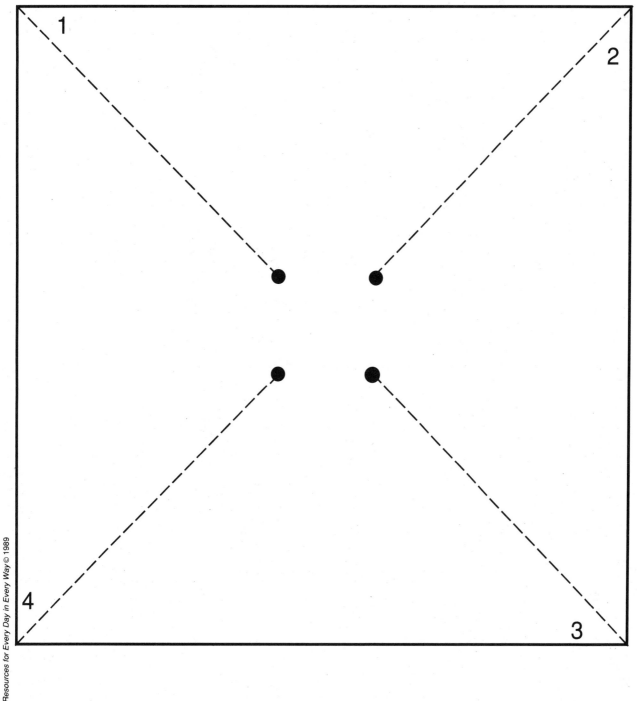

Name _____

 Unfinished Birthday Cake

How old are you? Draw the correct number of candles.
Color the cake.

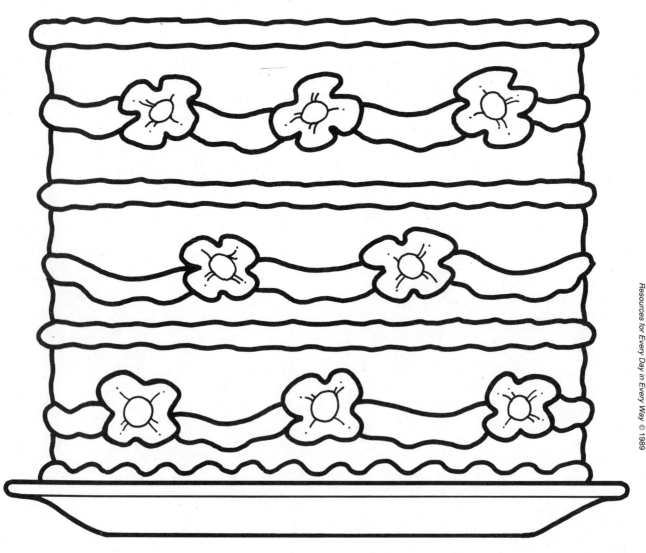

Resources for Every Day in Every Way

Index

Recipes for Crafts and Creations: 103–106

Bubble Solution, 105
Candles, 105
Clay #1, 105
Clay #2, 105
Collage Paste, 105
Face Paint, 105
Fingerpaint #1, 105
Fingerpaint #2, 105
Glowing Garden, 106
Papier Mâché, 106
Playdough #1, 106
Playdough #2, 106
Soap Suds Snow, 106
Snow Paint, 106

Recipes for Snacks and Meals: 107–117

Ants on a Log, 109
Apple Crisp, 109
Apple Sailboats, 109
Astronaut Roll-ups, 109
Baby's Applesauce, 109
Baked Apples, 109
Banana Coconut Snowmen, 109
Bendable Biscuits, 110
Butter, 110
Celery Boats, 110
Cereal Balls, 110
Cereal Snack Sacks, 110
Christmas Cookies, 110
Circus Popcorn, 110
Corn on the Cob, 111
Curds and Whey, 111
Dinosaur's Salad, 111
Edible Peanut Butter Playdough, 111
Eggnog, 111
Egg Yolk Cookie Paint, 111
Fingerfood Friends, 111
Fingerpaint Pudding, 112
Fourth of July Fruit Cup, 112
French Toast, 112
Fresh Fruit Salad, 112

Garden Salad, 112
Garlic Bread, 112
Gelatin Cubes, 112
Hot Chocolate, 112
Humpty Dumpty Eggs, 113
Individual Pizzas, 113
Latkes, 113
Lentil Soup, 113
Miss Cindy's Favorite Gingerbread People, 113
Miss Faraday's Stone Soup, 113
Monkey Sandwiches, 114
No-Bake Yummies, 114
Old-fashioned Lemonade, 114
Parlor Pack Ice Cream, 114
Perfect Peanut Butter Cookies, 114
Personalized Pretzels, 114
Pooh's Pancakes, 115
Popsicles, 115
Pudding Tarts, 115
Pumpkin Pie, 115
Pumpkin Seeds, 115
Quickest Bread, 115
Rainbow Toast, 116
Shape Kabobs, 116
S'Mores, 116
Snow Cones, 116
Spaghetti and Meatballs, 116
Sprouting Sprouts, 116
Strawberry Milkshakes, 116
Trail Mix, 117
Witch's Brew, 117
Yogurt Drink, 117

Reproducible Worksheets and Patterns: 119–219

Abraham Lincoln, 183
Animal Homes, 211
Baby Animals, 199
Baby's Diaper, 201
Balloons for the Clown, 188
Bat Pattern, 145
Bells, Balls, Stars, and Candy Canes, 166
Brother to Sister Maze # 1, 146

Bunny Headband, 197
Button Bunny, 195
Calico Cat, 156
Certificates, 150
Chef's Hat, 182
Christmas Stocking Pattern, 167
Christmas Tree, 168
Circus Patterns, 186
Clock and Mouse Pattern, 178
Clock Lotto, 179
Complete the Houses, 151
Corn for the Chickens, 204
Counting Animals, 210
Counting Coins, 216
Cow Pattern, 202
Daytime-Nighttime, 180
Dinosaur and Leaves Pattern, 213
Dot-to-Dot Food, 193
Dot-to-Dot Stegosaurus, 215
Dot-to-Dot Teepee, 152
Dreidel Pattern, 165
Easter Eggs, 198
Elephant Parade, 187
Fall Favorites, 140
Family Members, 148
Find the Toys, 162
Fingerpuppets with Feelings, 136
Follow the Path, 194
From Tadpole to Frog, 206
Giant Easter Egg, 196
Goldfish Bowl, 155
Goldfish Pattern, 159
Halloween Patterns, 143–144
Hand Puppet Pattern, 163
Handprints, 212
Hats for Snowmen, 173
Hidden Butterflies and Caterpillars, 205
Hidden Halloween Ghosts, 141
House Pattern, 149
Irish Flag, 191
Lacing Shoe Pattern, 175
Living and Nonliving Things, 184
Lost Toys, 171
Lucky Charms, 189

Menorah, 164
Mittens, 176
My Mirror, 132
On, Under, Next To, and
   In Front Of, 135
Ornament Patterns, 169
Pig Pattern, 203
Pinwheel, 217
Rattles for Babies, 200
Safety Signs, 185
Santa Star Pattern, 170
Schoolbus, The, 131
Shamrock Pattern, 190
Shape-a-Picture, 142
Sister to Brother Maze #2, 147
Snowflake Pattern, 174
Space Shapes, 209
Spot, 157
Teddy Bear, 160
Thanksgiving Patterns, 153–154
Three-Heart Shamrock, 192
Toy Patterns, 161
Train and Engineer, 208
Turtle Pattern, 158
Tyrannosaurus Rex Puppet, 214
Unfinished Birthday Cake, 218
Weather Chart, 137
Weather Pictures, 138–139
What's Missing? 133–134
Wheels, 207
Winter Clothes and Summer
   Clothes, 177
Winter Wonders, 172
Workers and Tools, 181

Songs, Rhymes, and Fingerplays: 57–101

ABC Song, 59
A-hunting We Will Go, 59
Aiken Drum, 59
Airplane, 59
America the Beautiful, 59
Animal Fair, The, 59
Animal Poem, 59
Ants Go Marching, The, 60
Apple Tree, 60
A-tisket, A-tasket, 60
August Heat, 60
Baa, Baa, Black Sheep, 60
Baby Bumblebee, 60
Baby Grows, 60
Baby's Toys, 61
Bear Went Over the Mountain,
   The, 61

Beehive, 61
Bingo, 61
Bingo's Doghouse, 61
Blastoff, 61
Blow a Balloon, 62
Bow Belinda, 62
Bow-wow Says the Dog, 62
Brother, Come and Dance
   with Me, 62
Bunny, 62
Bus Song, The, 62
Buttercups and Daisies, 63
Bye Baby Bunting, 63
Can You Show Me How the
   Farmer? 63
Carpenter, 63
Caterpillar, 63
Chickamy, Craney, Crow, 63
Chimney, The, 63
Choo-choo Train, 64
Christmas Is Coming, 64
Christmastime, 64
Clapping, Clapping, Softly
   Clapping, 64
Clap with Me, 64
Clementine, 64
Clocks, 64
Cobbler, Cobbler, 64
Cock-a-doodle-doo! 64
Counting Balls, 65
Creeping Indians, 65
Dancing Leaves, 65
Days of the Week, 65
Dentist, 65
Diddle, Diddle, Dumpling, 65
Did You Ever See a Lassie? 65
Dig a Little Hole, 65
Ding, Dong Bell, 65
Dinosaurs, 65
Don't Let the Dragons Get You, 66
Don't Worry If Your Job
   Is Small, 66
Donut Song, 66
Down by the Station, 66
Do Your Ears Hang Low? 66
Dragon Hunt, 66
Eenie, Meenie, Minie, Moe, 67
Eensy, Weensy Spider, 67
Evening Is Coming, The, 67
Eye Winker, 67
Farmer, 67
Farmer in the Dell, The, 67
Fee, Fie, Foe, Fum, 68
Fine Family, 68

Finger Band, 68
Fingers, Fingers Everywhere 68
Firefighter, 68
Fireflies, 68
Five Big Elephants, 68
Five Big Indians, 68
Five Birthday Candles, 69
Five Funny Speckled Frogs, 69
Five Huge Dinosaurs, 69
Five Kittens, 69
Five Little Babies, 69
Five Little Bears, 69
Five Little Bells, 70
Five Little Chickens, 70
Five Little Clowns, 70
Five Little Ducks, 70
Five Little Easter Rabbits, 70
Five Little Farmers, 71
Five Little Leaves, 71
Five Little Magnets, 71
Five Little Mice, 71
Five Little Monkeys Jumping on
   the Bed, 71
Five Little Monkeys Swinging in
   a Tree, 71
Five Little Pilgrims, 72
Five Little Presents, 72
Five Little Pumpkins, 72
Five Little Puppies, 72
Five Little Seashells, 72
Five Little Snowmen, 72
Five Little Squirrels, 72
Five Little Valentines, 73
Five Pretty Easter Eggs, 73
Flower, The, 73
For He's (She's) a Jolly Good
   Fellow, 73
Four Little Monkeys, 73
Four Seasons, 73
Foxes in Their Den, 73
Frère Jacques (Are You
   Sleeping?), 74
Fuzzy Wuzzy, 74
Georgy Porgy, 74
Ghost, The, 74
Go In and Out the Window, 74
Golden Fishes, 74
Good Morning to You, 74
Good Night, 74
Grandmother's Glasses, 74
Grasshoppers, 74
Hammering, 75
Hands on Shoulders, 75
Hanukkah Candles, 75
Have You Ever Seen? 75

Resources for Every Day in Every Way

Head, Shoulders, Knees, and Toes, 75
Here Are My Lady's Knives and Forks, 75
Here Is Baby's Tossled Head, 75
Here's a Ball, 75
Here's a Cup of Tea, 75
Here's a Hill, 76
Here Sits a Monkey, 76
He's Got the Whole World, 76
Hey Diddle, Diddle, 76
Hey Lolly, Lolly, 76
Hickory Dickory Dock, 76
Higgety-Piggety, My Black Hen, 76
Hippety Hop to the Barber Shop, 76
Hokey Pokey, 76
Home on the Range, 77
Hot Cross Buns, 77
House, The, 77
Houses, 77
Humpty Dumpty, 77
Hush, Little Baby, 77
I Am a Fine Musician, 77
I Am an Elephant, 77
I Asked My Mother, 77
I Caught a Fish Alive, 78
I Eat My Peas with Honey, 78
If All the World Were Paper, 78
If I Were a Horse, 78
If You Are Happy and You Know It, 78
I Have Ten Little Fingers, 78
I Love Little Pussy, 78
I Love the Mountains, 78
I Love You, 78
I'm a Little Teapot, 79
I'm a Nut, 79
I'm Glad, 79
In a Cabin, 79
I Saw Three Ships, 79
I Touch, 79
It's Raining, It's Pouring, 79
I've Been Working on the Railroad, 79
Jack Be Nimble, 79
Jack-in-the-Box, 79
Jack-o'-Lantern, 80
Jack Spratt, 80
Jelly, 80
Jingle Bells, 80
Johnny Pounds with One Hammer, 80

Kangaroo, The, 80
Kite, A, 80
Kitten Is Hiding, 80
Knock at the Door, 81
Kum Ba Ya, 81
Lavender's Blue, 81
Lazy Mary, Will You Get Up?, 81
Leaves, 81
Left to the Window, 81
Let Everyone Clap Hands with Me, 81
Let Your Hands Go Clap, 81
Listening Time, 81
Little Bo-Peep, 82
Little Boy Blue, 82
Little Bunny Foo Foo, 82
Little Drops of Water, 82
Little Jack Horner, 82
Little Liza Jane, 82
Little Miss Muffet, 82
Little Mouse, 82
Little Nut Tree, 82
Little Peter Rabbit, 82
Little Sally Saucer, 83
Little Tom Tinker, 83
Little Tom Tucker, 83
London Bridge, 83
Long, Long Ago, 83
Looby Loo, 83
Love Somebody, Yes I Do, 83
Mabel, Mabel, 83
Make New Friends, 83
Mary Had a Little Lamb, 84
Mary Mack, 84
Mary Wore Her Red Dress, 84
Merrily We Roll Along, 84
Michael Finnegan, 84
Michael, Row the Boat Ashore, 84
Mistress Mary, Quite Contrary, 84
More We Get Together, The, 84
Muffin Man, The, 84
Mulberry Bush: Version One, 85
Mulberry Bush: Version Two, 85
Mulberry Bush: Version Three, 85
My Bicycle, 85
My Bonnie, 85
My Dreydl, 85
My Father Owns the Butcher Shop, 85

My Garden, 86
My Hands, 86
My Name, 86
My Tall Silk Hat, 86
My Turtle, 86
Noble Duke of York, 86
North Wind Doth Blow, The, 86
Oats, Peas, Beans, 86
O Christmas Tree, 87
Oh Dear, What Can the Matter Be? 87
Oh How Lovely Is the Evening, 87
Oh Where Has My Little Dog Gone? 87
Old Gray Cat, The, 87
Old King Cole, 87
Old MacDonald, 87
Old Mother Hubbard, 87
Old Woman and the Pig, 88
One Finger, One Thumb, Keep Moving, 88
One for the Money, 88
One Little Elephant, 88
One Misty, Moisty Morning, 88
One Potato, Two Potato, 88
One, Two, Buckle My Shoe, 88
One, Two, Three Little Witches, 88
Open Them, Shut Them, 88
Over in the Meadow, 89
Over the River and Through the Woods, 89
Paper of Pins, 89
Pat-A-Cake, 89
Paw-paw Patch, 89
Peanut Butter, 89
Pease Porridge Hot, 90
Phone Number Song, 90
Pitter-pat, 90
Playmates, 90
Police Officer, 90
Polly Put the Kettle On, 90
Polly Wolly Doodle, 90
Pop Goes the Weasel, 90
Pound Goes the Hammer, 90
Punchinello, 90
Question, 91
Rag Doll, 91
Rain on the Green Grass, 91
Rain, Rain, Go Away, 91
Ride a Cock Horse, 91
Right Hand, Left Hand, 91
Ring Around the Rosie, 91

Robin Redbreast, 91
Rock-a-bye Baby, 91
Rocket in My Pocket, A, 91
Roses Are Red, 91
Row, Row, Row Your Boat, 91
Rub-a-Dub-Dub, 91
Safety Belts, 91
Sailor Went to Sea, Sea,
    Sea, A, 92
Sally Go Round the Sun, 92
Santa, 92
Sea, The, 92
See-saw, Margery Daw, 92
Senses, 92
She'll Be Coming 'Round the
    Mountain, 92
Shoo Fly, 93
Simple Simon, 93
Sing a Song of Sixpence, 93
Six Little Ducks, 93
Skip to My Lou, 93
Sleep, Baby, Sleep, 93
Sleepy Fingers, 93
Snail, The, 94
Snowflakes, 94
Snowmen, 94
Solomon Grundy, 94
Somebody Loves You, 94
Something About Me, 94
Spin a Coin, 94
Starlight, Star Bright, 94
Stop, Look, and Listen, 94
Swing Them, 94
Swinging, 94
Tall and Small, 95

Teddy Bear, 95
Ten Brave Firefighters, 95
Ten Fat Turkeys, 95
Ten in the Bed, 95
Ten Little Indians, 95
Ten Little Soldiers, 95
Ten Little Witches, 96
Ten Workers, 96
Thanksgiving Friends, 96
There's Music in a
    Hammer, 96
There Was a Crooked
    Man, 96
There Was an Old
    Woman, 96
This Is the Church, 96
This Is the Circle That Makes
    My Head, 96
This Is What I Can Do, 96
This Little Calf, 97
This Little Clown, 97
This Little Pig, 97
This Old Man, 97
Three-cornered Hat, The, 97
Three Little Kittens, 97
Thumbkin Says, "I'll Dance," 97
Tiger Walk, 97
"To Bed! To Bed!" Says
    Sleepyhead, 97
To Market, 98
Tomorrow's the Fair, 98
Toot! Toot! 98
To School, 98
Touch My Hair, 98
Traffic Lights, 98

Turkey, The, 98
Twinkle, Twinkle, Little Star, 98
Two Little Blackbirds, 98
Two Little Eyes, 98
Two Little Hands Go Clap,
    Clap, Clap, 98
Two Little Hands So Clean
    and Bright, 98
Two Little Houses, 99
Under the Spreading Chestnut
    Tree, 99
Unfortunately, 99
Up a Step, 99
Valentine's Good Morning, 99
Valentine, 99
Very Nicest Place, The, 99
Warm Hands, 99
Way Down South, 99
Wee Willie Winkie, 99
We Wish You a Merry
    Christmas, 99
When Johnny Comes Marching
    Home, 99
Where Is Thumbkin? 100
Whisky, Frisky, 100
White Coral Bells, 100
Who Feels Happy? 100
Wiggle, 100
Will You Be My Valentine? 100
Wind, The, 100
Witch's Haunted House, The, 101
Woodchuck, 101
Yankee Doodle, 101
Young Lady of Lynn, A, 101
Zoo, The, 101

About the Authors

Faraday Burditt De la Camara is presently directing the early childhood program at the American School of Madrid, Spain. She has previously taught English as a second language, preschool, and learning disabled children at the Rabat American School in Morocco. Ms. Burditt holds a B.A. in modern languages and an M.A. in curriculum and instruction. She is the mother of four trilingual children.

Cynthia Holley has 15 years experience teaching in classrooms for preschool, kindergarten, first grade, and special education students. She holds master's degrees in early childhood education and special education. She has served as a consultant to special education and early childhood education programs in the United States and Europe. Ms. Holley is currently a part-time instructor for Central Piedmont Community College, Charlotte, North Carolina. She often field-tests early childhood activities and strategies with her two preschool sons. She is also the author of *Holiday Stories* and *Bilingual Babies.*

Both authors conduct in-service training for the early childhood education program described in *Every Day in Every Way,* and they welcome inquiries.